FROM POVERTY TO
PRINCIPAL

A Guide to Promote Equity
and Student Advocacy

ANNETHA JONES

Published by:
Before You Publish – Book Press
Addison, Texas

Cover Designs: Rod Rudder
Cover Photo: Tamara Knight Photography

Published and printed in the United States of America

First Edition
ISBN-13: 978-0-578-89667-0
ISBN-10: 0-578-89667-0

Jones, Annetha
From Poverty to Principal – First edition

www.annethajones.com

FROM POVERTY TO
PRINCIPAL

A Guide to Promote Equity
and Student Advocacy

ANNETHA JONES

BeforeYouPublish Book Press™
———— We Publish Books ————
Addison, Texas

Contents

Acknowledgements

I must begin by thanking some amazing people for their unyielding support of me as I wrote this book. First, my husband and best friend, Cletis, who has always supported my personal and professional endeavors, unequivocally believes in me and unceasingly encourages me to pursue my goals. I am also so very thankful for my children, Jada and Marcus, who are truly my gifts from God and my source of daily inspiration.

My big brother, Rev. Dr. Isaac Williams, thank you for always being there and for the great advice. You have inspired me to continue my journey and reach for higher heights. Your prayers and belief in me have encouraged me tremendously. Ms. Dorothy Holley, I can't say enough about the wisdom you have imparted and the great advice you continuously provide me. Thank you, Rev. Dr. Williams and Ms. Holley, for the countless hours you both spent reviewing passages as I completed my book and for un-selfishly giving of your time. I appreciate you both more than you will ever know.

To my friend and coach, Dr. Stem Sithembile Malhatini, thank you for being an inspiration and for your continuous guidance and encouragement. My quest to complete this book was enhanced because of your advice.

I particularly want to thank my mother for allowing me to share her personal and confidential financial information in my book.

Finally, there are many others who supported me, and out of fear of forgetting someone, I would like to thank all my family and friends who supported me through this endeavor.

I appreciate each and every one of you.

INTRODUCTION

In this book, I will take you on a journey from my childhood experiences, into my adulthood. I will share strengths, vulnerabilities, and how my life events have continued to propel me to promote educational advocacy for Black and Brown students. I resolve to share my deliberate efforts and experiences of going *From Poverty to Principal*. Further, I will transparently impart personal and professional strategies to assist students of color on how to avoid common pitfalls as they navigate through the educational system. Although I certainly do not proclaim to have every solution, as a retired principal, I have been explicitly privy to direct knowledge to some of the inequities some students of color experience.

Clearly, there are many exceptional educational systems with a **tremendous** number of dedicated, caring, and concerned educators who are an integral force in combating inequalities.

Yet, with all the positives, we must continue to ensure that our students of color are afforded unabridged access and equitable opportunities to more rigorous courses. Therefore, I shall provide specific suggestions and advice as it relates to overcoming various obstacles our students of color face.

I am hopeful that this information will benefit parents, students, and teachers who are in pursuit of equality for all students. Additionally, suggested strategies will be provided to promote self-advocacy as students work towards their post-secondary education and careers.

I believe it is the villages obligation to work meticulously to prepare, support, and expose our students of color to exceptional educational experiences. Further, I will discuss how the creation and implementation of mentoring programs and co-curricular activities can be utilized to entice students to embrace educational challenges. Let's work to make sure all students are abreast of the amazing opportunities awaiting them. I welcome you to continue this journey with me.

"Anyone who has ever struggled
with poverty knows how extremely
expensive it is to be poor."

❧

James Baldwin

CHAPTER 1

You Get to Eat for Free, but You'll Have to Pay

As the start of my ninth-grade school year approached, I was oblivious to what lay ahead—a situation laced with limitations within an educational system responsible for providing me with a quality education and, ultimately, higher learning. Once at school, I learned I had been placed in a class not conducive to expanding my intellect.

It was the year 1978. I was a young, bright eyed, energetic African American girl, bursting with excitement and apprehension about entering high school. I welcomed the various adventures awaiting me there. As I prepared for my first day of school, selecting the perfect outfit was important. However, my financial resources were limited, and my wardrobe, or lack thereof, was scarce. After several minutes of contemplating, I was finally able to pair a two-piece ensemble together, which placed a faint smile on my face. Although my clothing choices may have been subpar, I took a great deal of pride in my appearance. Education was not at the forefront of discussions in my home, but oddly enough, I relished school and the extracurricular activities associated with it. Actually, I preferred being at school and enjoyed learning. As a result, I was seldom absent.

Although not always equitable, educational establishments were not a variable in my life, they were a constant. Thankfully, I was gifted with a thirst to learn and blessed with a protective aura from God.

The first day of school had finally arrived, and I was ecstatic. As I entered school, my gait was rapid and quite synchronized. However, my nerves consumed me, my stomach was in a knot, and my heart palpitated quickly, yet I refused to allow my apprehension to dampen the excitement of this newfound opportunity to learn and grow. While I was not an honor student, it was extremely important for me to prioritize my schoolwork and maintain satisfactory grades, as well as show respect for authority figures.

Immediately upon arriving at school, I sought out my friends. Once together, we discussed schedules, teachers, and lunch time, while barely containing our overzealous freshman enthusiasm. The day was off to a fantastic start. Then, after being in a brief state of naive adolescent utopia, I strolled into my math class where I found a sea of Black and Brown faces. When we congregated together, we felt an extra layer of peace and security in our southern town in Florida where it was not uncommon for people of color to experience blatant racism. In the past, I was usually placed in classes not nearly as diverse as I would have liked, with the dominant race being that of Caucasian students. Our school demographics was predominantly Caucasian with a relatively small number of students of color, which made this exceptionally monochromatic class highly unusual. Consequently, I ascertained, with all of us students of color in this one class, meant that something was amiss.

I glanced around the classroom trying to locate an unoccupied seat. The tardy bell had not sounded; however, the teacher, Mr. Smith, had positioned himself in front of the classroom. Mr. Smith appeared a bit apprehensive while anxiously waiting for the bell to sound. The majority of students were meandering around the room, cheerfully talking.

I ignored the rambunctious activities and continued searching for an empty seat near the front. Once I located a desk I would be claiming for the next forty-five minutes, I glided into the chair. Intense thoughts raced through my mind about the curriculum of this mathematics course.

Most of the students were talking amongst themselves about their complete and utter excitement as it related to being placed in the class with familiar faces and childhood friends. Their focus was on socializing rather than questioning the unusual makeup of our class. On the other hand, I remained perplexed on why this class was listed on my schedule. I arrived at the conclusion there had been a mistake, assuring myself, the teacher would correct it.

Finally, the bell sounded. Our teacher, Mr. Smith, was quite young, perhaps in his early twenties, and this was undoubtedly his first teaching assignment based on his body language. After Mr. Smith quieted the students, he introduced himself and began by reviewing the course syllabus and addressed routine questions intermittently. When he finished reviewing the syllabus, it was apparent the cognitive expectations were low. Several of the course requirements he outlined were similar to those I had completed during elementary school. I surmised that the class was a below-average mathematics course. Utterly clear to me was, I did not belong there, nor did many of the other students, and I planned to be removed.

When the class period ended, I meandered to the teacher's desk and inquired about why I had been placed in what appeared to be a class beneath my level. To my astonishment and dismay, the teacher stated I was there because I was a recipient of free or reduced lunch.

I did not know the academic placement process, nor the state laws governing school policies; however, I certainly knew it was unacceptable. My most immediate thought was, *I've been placed in this low-level phase one mathematics class because my mother can't afford to pay for my lunch.* I was not placed in the class because I needed extra support in math nor because my academic records had been thoroughly reviewed and the consensus was that this class would be the best fit for me. I was not in the class because it would help challenge me to reach my fullest potential. I was placed in this class simply because my mother was poor.

Mr. Smith insisted I would not be permitted to change my schedule because the class was designed specifically for students who were on the free or reduced lunch program. In retrospect, I venture to say, perhaps this inexperienced teacher was not supposed to share that confidential information with me. Because I continued to press him on the issue, he kindly instructed me to speak with the administration or guidance counselors about being removed.

I swiftly located a person of authority who could transfer me into the proper class. I was embarking upon the uncharted territory of being an advocate for myself. I had never utilized my voice to this extent at school before, but I recognized the necessity and there was no other recourse. I was determined to resolve this issue.

To my dismay, I was informed by the administrator that I would not be transferred from the class. I absolutely declined to accept that response so immediately after school, I hurried home and informed my mother of the experience I'd had at school. I then pleaded with her to have me removed from the course. Although I was adamant she would assist me with this predicament, she was not usually involved in my education. She relied on me to ensure everything was in order at school. Fortunately, I was able to perform and maintain my grades at an acceptable level with minimal parental support.

Over the years, I thought intensely about my mother's lack of involvement in my education. I arrived at the conclusion it stemmed from her leaving high school before finishing, although many years later, she enrolled in night school and completed the process. Not attaining a higher level of education is one of the reasons why my mother's income was insufficient to support our small family. I was the only child born between my mother and my father's untraditional union. My parents never married, nor did they stay in contact with each other, therefore, I did not establish a relationship with my father until I was an adult.

During my middle school years, my cousin Luke moved from Georgia to live with us because he, too, faced instability and poverty issues. Although I was happy to have Luke come live with us, I knew it would be even more financially difficult as we barely had the essentials for our day-to-day living. As a matter of fact, during this time period in my life, my mother only earned minimum wage which was about $2.30 per hour. Even so, my mother was surprised her income was a factor in me being placed in a substantially low-level math class.

I told my mother the steps I had already taken to advocate for myself. Because I was adamant about being removed from the class, she proceeded to the school the next day. Once there, she insisted that my schedule be changed instantly.

During the late 70s, classes were established by "intellectual" phases. Phase one was the lowest phase and phase four was the highest. Although I did not presume to be prepared for phase four level math curriculum, I certainly knew that phase one was far below my potential.

After my mother spoke with the administration, I was removed from the phase one placement and promptly relocated into a phase three class. Although the new class provided a phase level that was higher than the previous placement, I was certain this transfer was not a strategic move to challenge my intellect but rather to appease my mother.

Once I was transferred, I continued to think about the other students who were left behind in the math class. I wondered if the other students would advocate for themselves or plead with their parents to have them transferred the same way I had. One student in particular was of great concern to me, my cousin, Luke. I pleaded with my mother to get him out of the class as well. However, he was adamant that he wanted to remain there because it would be a surefire way for him to earn an easy A. I hoped my mother would force him to transfer. Unfortunately, because she was not sure of his intellectual capacity, and because he demanded to stay there, he remained in the course. Although I was only a teen, this saddened me greatly because I knew this was not a good placement for him. He certainly had more potential than what the class offered him.

Of course, at that time, I didn't know how to determine intelligence levels, but I knew he was capable of more simply based on our day-to-day conversations. I firmly believe because he stayed in that class, it fostered his already low expectations for himself. The lower phased, unchallenging math course did not expose him to a curriculum that would foster his mind to expand or serve as a motivational tool for him to strive to do his best in school. That class was another crutch that potentially hindered Luke's motivation and possibly some of his op-portunities. The course certainly did not push him towards attending college. Unfortunately, he became another Black male statistic who narrowly finished high school and soon after, found himself making poor decisions. As a result, he struggled emotionally and financially once he became an adult.

Over the years, I often thought about this situation. I do not have concrete statistics from that class, of course, but I distinctly recall many of my classmates who were placed there, continued on that track of low-level courses throughout the duration of high school. Sadly, a large majority of those students did not pursue post-secondary learning after high school.

Though only an adolescent, I was keenly aware there were racial and socio-economic issues prompting this course to be established in the first place. Even though this experience was unpleasant for me, I am convinced it ignited an awareness for me to become more alert and cognizant of my educational environment. It was an awakening of sorts, to look at education differently and deeper. I learned to accept that I could not solely rely on those who worked in the school system to ensure my educational needs were a priority.

Even after the negative experience, I still wanted so badly to believe that all the adults at the school were there as a part of the village to protect the student body. However, despite the many faculty and staff who displayed great care for all of us, there were others who did not make efforts to deposit positivity into students of color, treating us differently from our white counterparts. As much as I wanted to ignore it, I could feel the difference in treatment, if by nothing else, their tones. This was our reality, and, in many instances, it still is.

"We have a powerful potential in our youth, and we must have the courage to change old ideas and practices so that we may direct their power toward good ends."

Mary McLeod Bethune

CHAPTER 2

Planning is Good, Action is Better

I sincerely and explicitly believe my erroneous ninth-grade course placement propelled me to become a staunch advocate for myself much sooner than the natural expectation. The experience was the beginning of me advocating for myself. After being removed from the low-level math class, I paid close attention to my course placements and whenever I felt I was not placed correctly, or that another class would suit me better, I spoke up about it. Additionally, I became more aware of how the adults spoke to me and my classmates and, if necessary, I would respectfully question their motives in particular situations. Most students were unaware that such significant issues existed, nor should they have had to concern themselves with such things as proper course placements. Consequently, I knew it was going to be up to me to ensure that I prepared myself for graduation and beyond. Therefore, I formulated a success plan for myself at a young age. Of course, my plan was not detailed or structured. Nor did I know the intricate elements of professional goal setting. However, intuitively, my plan consisted of getting a part-time job to assist with my financial needs and committing to participate in extracurricular activities at school. I surmised that being actively involved would motivate me to maintain focus.

Furthermore, I intentionally surrounded myself with likeminded students. As a result, I joined the Student Government Association and Delta Omega, which was the only club on campus designed specifically to support minorities. I also made the basketball team and fostered robust relationships. My coach was nurturing, while holding the players to high expectations. She served as a surrogate mother to each of us while embracing our differences. Our socioeconomic status only mattered to her if she recognized a player was unable to purchase required gear, if so, she would then donate athletic wear she had received from a vendor to a player in need. I relished being at practice so much that even when ill, I refused to forgo basketball practice because it served as a comfortable haven of routine and structure.

Confronted with profound obstacles, coupled with the lack of financial security as a child, forced me to work to overcome the odds and break a vicious cycle. Unfortunately, that was not the case for many of my peers. I witnessed several students from my high school cohort succumb to their underprivileged and oppressed circumstances. I almost spiraled into those undesirable conditions. However, I was so determined to elevate my circumstances, I sought a workers permit at the tender age of thirteen in order to secure part-time employment. I was ultimately granted the permit, began working, and although not substantial, the meager income certainly helped.

As a result of my efforts to improve my circumstances, I graduated high school, attended the local community college, then transferred to Florida AM University (FAMU) and my final educational institution matriculation was to Nova Southeastern University (NOVA), where I received a master's and an Educational Specialist degree. While this may seem as if it were a seamless process, it was not without the struggles of financial burdens and logistical challenges. Getting accepted and enrolling into the community college was not a difficult process because I lived at home. Transitioning into FAMU was more complex, both financially and logistically, as I would now have to pay to live on campus.

Because my mother was not familiar with the college application process, hence, I was on my own to navigate this unknown territory. Fortunately, I had mentors who assisted me along the way by offering solid advice. This support system ignited my interest in mentoring programs, which I created and implemented after becoming a teacher and an administrator. I will share those programs and the importance of mentors for our youths later.

Upon completing community college, I applied for a Pell Grant and was unexpectedly denied. I was devastated. I found the rejection difficult to accept, considering the financial status of my mother. Attending FAMU was completely contingent upon being approved for the Pell Grant, as I would not be able to enroll without financial assistance. I was uncertain if I could apply twice for the grant, but instinctively I had to try. Subsequently, I did so immediately and thankfully, I was approved on the second attempt.

The confirmation I would receive assistance from the grant, in conjunction with the savings I had hoarded from my part-time jobs, gave me confidence to prepare for my new residence on the campus at FAMU, one of the best HBCUs (historically black colleges and universities) in this country, considering the overall college experience. I attained cum laude academic status and shortly after graduating, I relocated to Miami, Florida for my initial teaching assignment.

Once there, I taught high school while simultaneously attending Nova Southeastern University to earn a master's in Computer Applications. I continued at NOVA and received my Educational Specialist degree in School Leadership, hence my career as an educational leader. It was imperative to perform my absolute best. Therefore, I graduated with a 4.0 grade point average in both my master's and Educational Specialist degree programs. Subsequently, NOVA officials requested use of my practicum (a written report to show theoretical concepts within a practical frame-work) for their national data base as an example for others.

Unquestionably, FAMU proved to be a remarkable experience that is indelibly en-grained in my memory. Instantly upon arriving, I was confident I had made the correct choice. That decision confirmed, with a level of certainty, that I would successfully obtain my college degree. I resolved that I was not departing without my credentials.

The initial and most prevalent observation I made upon my arrival was the abundance of black and brown faces in all of my classes. But this time, my experience was in complete and total contrast to the one in the ninth grade. It was abundantly clear through conversations and observations that the students at FAMU *wanted* to be in those classes and so did I. We all desired to be with students and faculty who looked like us. We were there because we wanted an education from a facility where there was no concern of being mistreated or excluded because of the color of our skin. We were there because we could leisurely walk through the campus and not focus on the possibility of our character being attacked or being belittled based on our race or culture. We were there because courageous trailblazers had gone before us and paved a path for us to have this higher learning opportunity.

Students were embraced, challenged, and supported beyond anything I could have ever imagined. It was a welcomed and unimaginable awakening. The level of faculty encouragement at FAMU was outstanding. The professors took a vested interest in each student while providing rigorous and challenging cur-riculums. We were forced to think critically, which prepared us to excel in a world that often made it difficult for students of color to advance professionally. FAMU students often chatted amongst each other that we were pressed to excel far above mediocrity because people of color must work twice as hard as our counter-parts.

I became acquainted with numerous extraordinary people from all walks of life.

Some were from the lower socioeconomic background like me, some were middle class, while others were wealthy or at least "well to do." Incidentally, one of my classmates was the son of a US House of Representatives member. I had never networked with anyone of this caliber before, so I found it quite intriguing.

I would be remiss not to share the astounding experiences that occurred during my time at FAMU. My hope is to encourage college-bound students to visit, and perhaps ultimately consider attending, an HBCU.

At FAMU, classes were fairly small, and exuberance lingered in the air. Many of the students shared a great deal of common interest, such as receiving a solid education while feeling valued. The campus cafeteria had delectable and scrumptious food. Each day after breakfast, lunch, or dinner, students were sure to see a gathering in front of the cafeteria and on the "set." The set was the casual hangout scene for students. There, we were mesmerized by Greek step shows and the clusters of students relishing the company of their peers on any given day.

There were countless activities at our disposal. For example, we engaged in the best football game escapades and we were rarely concerned with the winning record. For many of us, the games served as another gathering location for us to celebrate our utter and complete love for FAMU. Another cohesiveness amongst us was how we marveled at the Marching 100 band. The band was so outstanding, we would sit in the blazing hot sun for hours on end, observing them practice.

An extracurricular highlight for me, par- ticularly, was the modeling group on campus called Couture. Modeling with this group proved to be a prudent decision because it fostered teamwork and, for me, confidence. In order to have a successful show, members formed bonds because between the onstage appearances, we were only allotted approximately sixty seconds, or sometimes less, to change our attire. It was necessary to have reliable teammates to pull this off.

During my initial year of modeling at FAMU, the renowned *Ebony Fashion Fair* Modeling extraordinaire troupe was our guest. Immediately following their show, a team member and I were approached by their representatives and asked if we would consider postponing school for a year to travel and model with them. I was so excited I could hardly catch my breath. However, after I calmed myself, I realized that leaving school for a year would jeopardize my graduation. Therefore, I respectfully declined the offer and it was one of the most difficult decisions I have ever had to make, but my education was priority. I had selected to major in education and was eager to teach and impact the lives of students in a positive manner.

Consequently, after graduation, I started my teaching career in Miami, Florida. Teaching, by far, was incomparable to any job I have ever held. I adored my students and was blessed to have wonderful relationships with them. As a matter of fact, my students, who are now adults, continue to call and visit with me. I valued all my students but was particularly interested and involved in the lives of the minority students, especially those with similar backgrounds to mine. I intentionally set my sights on serving as an African American female leader and role model to use that platform to encourage young adults of color to work towards overcoming poverty and its related obstacles.

Interestingly enough, many of my students repeatedly registered for multiple and various business courses I taught. A few of my students enrolled consecutively and actively participated in five of my classes; hard to believe but true. This further increased my awareness of the thirst and desire of minority students to be exposed to teachers who actually resembled them and have a keen awareness of the Black community.

Over the years, I have participated in numerous discussions about the relevance of students of various ethnicities being exposed to people who represent their race. Many of my students have expressed concern over the lack of Black and Brown educators. More strategic efforts must be made to bring diversity into education. Surely, this will serve as a means to eradicate some of the prejudice's students of color face far too frequently.

Unfortunately, from kindergarten through graduation, I had only four Black teachers, which is an incredibly limited number but more than many of my peers had experienced. Though, there were two consistent Black teachers throughout my high school years. One was deemed a dominant force in literature and taught some honors courses. I was determined to enroll in a literature course under her tutelage and eventually, I did. When she recited poetry, it was prolific, and easily commanded one's attention. On the other hand, her colleague dedicated a great deal of her time with students of color. She sponsored the only club on campus focusing on minority student issues. I spent countless hours in her classroom, before, during, and after school. I felt blessed to have a Black teacher who genuinely cared about me.

There was a small number of other Black teachers throughout my high school experience; however, they seldom remained at the school for any length of time. I speculate it was related to the lack of diversity in the school as that remains an issue.

I want to encourage all the young educators about to embark upon one of the most important and impressionable jobs in the world, to please reflect on your charge. In addition, position yourselves to help eradicate inequities in education. These problems have plagued minority students for centuries and unfortunately, some believe it should not garner any additional attention. Educators and members of the village must take responsibility to ensure all students are treated impartially, with equity as the standard.

Our nation has an insurmountable number of outstanding, caring, and dedicated educators—educators who vowed to embrace and teach all students without regard to their race, religion, creed, or color. It is essential that educators do not succumb to the pressures of those who hold on to stereotypes, oppressive behaviors, and racial biases. When educators treat all students equally when teaching, they are opening up opportunities for students to become more prepared for post-secondary learning, set their goals high, and not be limited because of the color of their skin or the prevalent and existing inequalities. Educators hold an enormous level of responsibility.

Students of all ethnicities yearn to be accepted and supported and students of color are no different. Unfortunately, they are often treated differently and face profound circumstances other students are not susceptible to. We must work collectively and strategically to change this fact and provide all students equal access to a fair and appropriate education.

Although the preceding narrative is a summary of my personal and specific educational experiences, the upcoming chapters will reveal firsthand, insightful knowledge and information to help students, parents, or educators become more alert to the sometimes blatant, and oftentimes, subtle racial inequalities existing in some educational systems. These systemic issues will not be eradicated magically. It will require strategic and deliberate planning in order to ensure that Black students are given every opportunity to grow in pedagogical institutions without the prevalent and insidious disease of racial inequality as a barrier.

Progressing "from poverty to principal" required me to utilize the methods I will share in this book. I show you how to avoid many of the trial and errors of navigating through the educational system I was exposed to, and/or unable to avoid, based on my specific circumstances. Ultimately, awareness, self-advocacy, and direct involvement will hinder and deflect most of the ill-intended aims.

"Empower yourselves with a good education, then get out there and use that education to build a country worthy of your boundless promise."

Michelle Obama

CHAPTER 3

Proper Course Placement Must be Deliberate

Upon becoming a principal, I became even more cognizant of how prevalent it is for large numbers of Black and Brown students to be placed in classes that do not challenge them or provide them with a productive struggle to advance academically. We must labor ambitiously to ensure our students are not placed in courses beneath their intellectual potential.

This chapter is especially significant to me as the content directly aligns with the first chapter, which is one of the primary reasons I felt it essential to write this book. Of course, there are other substantial reasons I share my story, and other relevant information, but that nineth grade erroneous class placement was the catalyst and a significant factor. After being placed in the subpar math course because of my low socio-economic status, I became fixated on preventing this from happening to other students, particularly students of color.

During my principalship, it became obvious that deliberate exertions towards appropriate academic placement for minority students was not always paramount. I essentially found that a limited number of Black and Brown students were being placed into the higher level and more rigorous courses. To the contrary, numerous capable minority students were assigned to basic classes. Upon analyzing the data closely, it was confirmed that many of those students would benefit from the productive struggle of accelerated courses.

At the middle school level, I began the process of reviewing academic data to ascertain students who may not have been correctly placed. While doing so, it was brought to my attention that some students of color were concerned about their reputation and being placed in honors courses wasn't the cool thing to do. Therefore, I worked to convince as many as possible it was best for them. To my astonishment, convincing them was more difficult than I had initially expected. Conceivably, some students did not want to accept the label of "honors" because their friends would think they were nerdy. In addition, some students simply were not accustomed to the lack of diversity those courses offered and obviously found their current situation more familiar and comfortable.

I witnessed one Black male student obstinately refuse to relocate to the new course when his schedule was changed to an advanced class. His tests scores were high and reflected it would benefit him to be relocated. Therefore, I personally made an effort to convince him this was best for him academically. Initially, when I approached him, he smiled and listened but as he realized the change was imminent, he became frustrated and more resistant. In the end, I bargained with him and convinced him to attempt the coursework and that if it proved too difficult, I would revisit the placement.

This scenario occurred in more than one instance. My takeaway from this was that it was even more imperative for minority students to be exposed to higher educational standards and more rigorous coursework as early as possible in order to eliminate the stigma some feel when propositioned with the challenge of higher-level courses. Higher-level placement needs to be normalized for our students of color and not be an anomaly.

Once I became principal at the high school level, course misplacement continued to be an issue. Therefore, I personally reviewed individual student data and made specific requests for minority students whose data revealed misplacement to be relocated into more rigorous classes. After speaking with numerous colleagues from various districts, I concluded that student misplacement was not uncommon. The explanations for inadequate placement ranged from unintentional errors, to the lack of attention to details. Either way, I was flabbergasted to discover that even with the use of modern technology to gather and analyze data, it was not an occasional issue but remained a common problem.

As a result of my disconcerting findings, I developed a strategy to target students for what I shall refer to as "fullest potential" placement. This meant I required statistical data to be utilized to drive a student's placement into the proper courses. Data, along with specific academic records and deliberate efforts, should be the primary driving force for placement for all students.

Conversations with other educators within and beyond our school district, although disturbing, revealed some students were not placed into higher-level classes solely because of their discipline record. By no stretch of the imagination should a student be placed into a lower-level class purely based on their prior history of exhibiting misconduct. Perhaps they exhibited misconduct because they were not being challenged. Perhaps they exhibited misconduct because they were placed into a homogenous group of other students who were not being held to high expectations either. Whatever the reason for an inadequate placement, there is no room for those types of erroneous mishaps.

My many years of experiences has shown me that the large majority of students will categorically rise to the level of expectations of the adults in authority. If students are held to low expectations, many will perform at that level. If students are challenged and expected to perform at an elevated level, most will work diligently and strive to meet the goal. I unequivocally believe in holding students, and the adults who teach them, to high standards. We are doing a disservice to the community at large if we do otherwise.

At one point during my second year as principal at the high school, I took a deep and meticulous review of students who had been unsuccessful on the state assessments even after several attempts. However, their data revealed they were absolutely capable of mastering the content with a strategic academic plan that would provide specific support in the areas where they struggled most. I dug a little further and found that many of these students were minority, and most had never been enrolled in an honors course. This was astonishing.

As a data-driven leader, I was convinced the data was factual but not consistently utilized to determine placement. My goal was for those capable students who had been repeatedly unsuccessful on the state assessments to be placed in honors courses where they would be held to much higher expectations. This intervention served as a means to prepare the students for mastering the content and ultimately, demonstrating proficiency or better on the state assessment. Our exertion to maximize the higher-level placement provided the students with opportunities for success.

I will never forget the facial expression one Black male displayed when I informed him he would be placed into an honors course. His eyes opened wide and he gasped. Then he said, "Me, Mrs. Jones, in an honors class... I've never had an honors class in my life." Disappointingly, he had reached upperclassman level and had never been enrolled into an accelerated course even though he was a bright young man. His home life was near catastrophic due to generational poverty and other tragic circumstances such as his father being incarcerated most of his life and his mother teetering on neglecting her children altogether. I recognized that he faced tremendous barriers, but I was determined to elevate his situation and help him see that he could change the trajectory of his life by becoming more vested in his education. I assured him that based on his academic records and tests data, he exhibited potential to be successful in an honors course as long as he put forth the effort. He was excited and once he began the class, he enthusiastically reported to me almost daily to update me on his progress. I was proud of him and he was equally and incredibly proud of himself. Without saying a word, I observed his beautiful smile and his strut as he walked across campus. The honors placement had become a quest, perhaps, he had never imagined as a possibility.

Deliberate placement efforts with students identified to be relocated to more rigorous courses continued. Some of my students were intimidated and a few outright resisted the more challenging courses because they were simply not accustomed to that level of intensity. They were afraid they would fail, or the coursework and assignments would be too difficult. With a little coercion, many of these students would reluctantly accept my recommendation. It gives me great pleasure to say most of the students did exceptionally well with the new challenges but unfortunately, there were a few who exhibited an unwelcome productive struggle and were not receptive to this new and foreign challenge of their potential. Still, I would much rather students have a productive struggle than not be challenged to their fullest potential at all.

I would be remiss not to acknowledge the placement efforts were a work in progress to eradicate ill-placements of minorities. Aggressive attempts to ensure all students were placed according to their potential were utilized. Regrettably, some may not have received the attention they deserved, as this task required a number of elements merging together.

It is essential for our Black and Brown students to have access to higher-level programs, no differently than their White counter parts. Therefore, it is imperative that parents, educators, and the entire village work to laboriously encourage students to enroll in these accelerated courses in an effort to push them to their full potential. Consequently, I will provide an explanation of various courses and programs more students of color must take advantage of more frequently.

Below, I share a detailed list for those who are not aware of the accelerated courses or program offerings available to your student. The following are specific programs available in the state and district in which I was a principal. Please note, school districts may vary in their program offerings.

HONORS COURSES

Honors courses are designed to be more challenging than basic courses and they weigh more heavily when it comes to enhancing the high school grade point average. The advantage of having a higher grade point average matters greatly when students are applying for acceptance into competitive colleges.

DUAL ENROLLMENT (DE)

Dual Enrollment courses are college classes students are enrolled in simultaneously while still in high school. Oftentimes, the school district will pay for these courses and provide the student with textbooks at no costs. The advantage is, these courses count towards a student's college degree, meaning, a student will spend less time in college after high school graduation because of the college credits received from passing these courses. This equates to spending less money on college tuition. In addition, dual enrollment classes are looked upon favorably by many colleges and universities, which is a benefit when submitting a college application. An extra advantage to taking a dual enrollment course is that the courses are most often worth 5.0 weighted credits, as opposed to the traditional 4.0 scale.

ADVANCED PLACEMENT (AP) COURSES

Advanced Placement (AP) courses are designed by a college board to give high school students an introduction to college-level courses. These courses will also assist in increasing the grade point average faster than taking traditional high school classes. In these classes, a great deal of course content and material are covered rather quickly. Colleges look favorably upon students who have taken AP courses because they are challenged with rigorous, college-level material and must pass an AP exam upon completion of the course in order to reap the full benefits. An extra advantage, like dual enrollment, is AP courses are most often worth 5.0 weighted credits as opposed to the traditional 4.0 scale. A student can earn a B in AP courses and still be able to potentially maintain a 4.0 grade point average in that course.

There are definite advantages to both dual enrollment and AP courses such as accelerated learning, college credits, and their appeal on the college application. Successful completion of a dual enrollment course automatically ensures college credit will be granted. Whereas, in addition to passing an AP course, students must also successfully pass an AP performance exam to earn college credits. Therefore, it is important to remember both are exceptional choices, but dual enrollment is a guaranteed credit as long as the course completion is successful. In addition, dual enrollment courses provide an avenue to save an enormous amount of time and money by those pursuing a post-secondary degree.

INDUSTRY CERTIFICATION

Let's face it, not all students, no matter how intelligent they are, will attend college. Therefore, I advise parents to listen carefully to your student when they express their post high school endeavors. Of course, as parents, it is our responsibility to steer them in the direction where they will receive the best education to find a career or gainful employment to provide for themselves. However, I have observed over the years some students who are adamant about not attending college, but instead, want to take up a trade or a skill. This is where the industry certifications can be especially useful. If the student's schedules are properly prepared, a student can leave high school with certification in a skilled area, i.e., culinary, digital, mechanical, etc. Oftentimes, these students are hired right out of high school and are paid reasonable salaries or wages.

It has been my experience that some students will take advantage of all of the above. I have seen many students enroll in Honors, DE, AP, and then for their electives, they will choose an industry certification program, whereas upon completion, they are qualified and eligible to become certified in a trade.

COURSE PLACEMENT PROCESS RECOMMENDATIONS

Parents, I would like to recommend a few key factors to help you get your students in courses that will challenge them, increase their grade point average, and increase their chances for post-secondary opportunities:

1. Each summer, prior to the start of school, request a conference with the guidance counselor to discuss your student's educational plan. Far too often, parents believe the school will ensure and assign the correct and most advantageous courses for their student. The fact is, when schedules are made, schools work to fill classes and although proper placement is the goal, minority students do not always receive detailed attention to their course placement.

2. It is imperative to ask lots of questions about the courses, the teachers, and the academic placement level. You have a right to discuss the appropriateness of each course and what is best or your student.

3. During your meeting with the guidance counselor, review your student's test scores and academic records. To be sure your student is on track for graduation, ask questions about the number of credits required for each school year. This is an indication of whether your student has been placed appropriately. If you don't understand the requirements or the process, ask for an explanation. It may even be necessary for your student

to take an online or summer school course to stay on track.

4. Encourage your student to attend before or after school tutor sessions as often as possible, even if they are doing well in their classes. This will help ensure they stay on solid footing. If your student is doing well, they should not be required to attend help sessions, but it's certainly not a bad idea, as attending can only enhance their knowledge.

Students of color deserve the same opportunities as their Caucasian counterparts so, the village must work collectively to encourage students to enroll in the courses I mentioned, even when they are resistant to doing so.

As stated prior, by enrolling in more rigorous courses, students can potentially graduate with a grade point average exceeding a 4.0. Unfortunately, during my tenure at the high school, there was not an abundance of Black and Brown students who were awarded this distinction at the graduation ceremonies. However, there is no reason why many more minority students should not take advantage of these opportunities. Through deliberate placement efforts, we can substantially increase the number of minority students who are enrolled and ultimately successful with this endeavor.

"We've got to work to save our children and do it with full respect for the fact that if we do not, no one else is going to do it."

Dorothy Height

CHAPTER 4

Due Process for All:
Disciplinary Strategies to
Avoid the Pitfalls

Without discipline, it is virtually impossible for learning to take place, and learning is certainly not maximized in the absence of discipline. Quite frankly, if classrooms lack discipline and structure, learning is hindered severely. Unfortunately, history has shown that when students of color commit infractions, the consequences following are often inequitable. Disciplinary consequences are inconsistently applied when assigned to Black and Brown students. Thus, the primary focus of this chapter is to provide information and suggestions on the disproportionate application of corrective strategies as it relates to students of color.

Based on my experiences as a former principal, I will suggest how to overcome unequal treatment and ultimately promote self-advocacy to circumvent excessive consequences. Students of all races will break school rules at some point. The problem is when minority students commit infractions, they overwhelmingly receive stiffer punishments. Often, students of color are suspended and/or expelled a great deal more than their counterparts. Clearly, suspensions or expulsions may be warranted at some point, according to the infraction, but many times are not equitable.

A couple of years ago, I elected to participate on the district's discipline committee. The desired outcome for the committee was to draft a districtwide discipline plan. Ultimately, the group was responsible for creating a document to specifically identify infractions and directly align them to the appropriate corrective strategies. The purpose of developing the document was to alleviate inconsistencies as it related to the application of punitive actions and to ensure consequences are more equitable for all students. However, to be clear, it is not the consequences that are inequitable in this district, or any other district, it was the decisions of individuals who inappropriately issued the corrective strategies.

Obviously, there are possibly many reasons for student misconduct. For some students, it may be the lack of structure in their classes or at home; for some, it may come from not feeling supported in school; and for others, it may be a temporary unruly adolescent stage. No matter their circumstances, all students deserve fair and equitable treatment if, and/or when, an infraction has been committed. Sadly, there have been students who, after numerous attempts to modify their behavior with multiple interventions, unfortunately succumbed to their situation. However, the overwhelming majority responded favorably to unconditional support and deliberate opportunities to correct their behavior.

I must emphasize the importance of students advocating for themselves, even in the simplest of forms, as it relates to direct or perceived unfair treatment or situations at school. Student advocacy is one of the most dominant strategies I repeatedly discuss throughout this book. By utilizing the suggested information below, it will serve as a guide to help avoid unnecessary disciplinary actions.

AVOIDING OUT-OF-SCHOOL SUSPENSIONS

Whenever possible, I worked to ensure my students did not receive an out-of-school suspension as a result of the students' corrective strategy. I vehemently believe that students stand a better chance at having a successful school year if they are able to remain in school. My first position as assistant principal of discipline was at a middle school, and upon accepting the position, I instantly recognized the suspension rate was disproportionally high for students of color.

I later, as principal, contemplated a plan to implement an in-school suspension (ISS) program. I also recognized that by establishing an in-school suspension program, it would drastically reduce out-of-school suspensions and enhance success opportunities for my students. It was important to provide them with every opportunity to remain in school, particularly for infractions that were not substantial. In-school suspension units were not provided by the school district at that time. Hence, I reallocated funds in the school budget with the purpose of supporting an in-school suspension unit. As a matter of fact, the area superintendent was so appreciative of the development of this unit she requested that I share with other principals how the program was established, in an effort to reduce out-of-school suspensions district-wide.

At the onset of establishing the in-school suspension program, I gathered data to ascertain the types of infractions being committed, the time of day, the location of the offenses, and how often violations were occurring by our most frequent rule breakers. To my dismay, I found on some occasions, minority students were being coerced when they were already angry, which often led to them making even poorer decisions. This led to the infractions being compounded. My immediate objective was to communicate with the adults involved to offer support and other strategies for handling these volatile situations.

The majority of the time, I was successful in encouraging the adults to reconsider their actions but unfortunately, there were instances when some would take no accountability. Some teachers did not consider these types of discussions an acceptable use of their time, nor did they want to reciprocate in the conversations. This prompted me to think even deeper about the obstacles students of color were confronted with while at school.

I must express that an overwhelming majority of the teachers extended themselves enormously to support their students. As an administrator and a parent, I appreciated those faculty and staff members tremendously. It was evident our students valued them as well. Often, these were the teachers our students migrated to frequently. It gave me great joy to know these teachers were contributing to the success of the village.

Foremost, it is imperative parents hold in-depth conversations with their students about the importance of protecting themselves by avoiding disciplinary issues altogether. However, if students are addressed for discipline issues, there are several strategies I implore parents to emphasize to their students in order to minimize the consequences. Below, I provide firsthand experiences and suggestions on how to minimize consequences and avoid pitfalls occurring far too frequently for students of color.

Speaking directly to the students:

1. If a teacher, staff, or faculty member directs you to the office for discipline issues, follow their instructions precisely. Although you may be distressed, it is vital to not allow the situation to escalate by taking a detour.

2. Upon arriving at the office, you may be asked to write a statement related to the circumstances. I highly recommend you respectfully request to call your parents prior to writing the statement. Involving your parents in all disciplinary issues from the onset is critical to ensuring you have an extra layer of support. Undoubtedly, when parents are involved from the onset, the administration will perhaps proceed more cautiously. Hence, this will further provide you with a better opportunity of a positive outcome and/or ensure the consequences are judicious.

3. Next, the administrative team will most likely question you whether your parents

are present or not. Even if you committed the offense, do not forget you would be better suited to sit quietly and respectfully until you are able to speak with your parents. In doing so, you minimize your likelihood of becoming victim to a false support system. If you committed the offense, you absolutely deserve consequences for your actions. Yet remember, consequences are not always given out equitably. A small offense could land you at the alternative center simply based on your responses. This is an instance where relying on a support team for minority students is particularly important.

4. If you are assigned an in-school suspension for your infraction, it is indisputably to your advantage to attend. During ISS, you are permitted the opportunity to complete your coursework for that day. If you fail to appear for an in-school suspension without a valid excuse, the likely recourse is out-of-school suspension. I highly advise you avoid missing for this reason. In addition, please remember the time you spend in ISS gives you an opportunity to stay abreast of your classwork and not fall behind in your academic studies, hence making your transition back to class much smoother.

CLASSROOM ISSUES

Although there are an astronomical number of outstanding, caring, and nurturing teachers, there are also those who do not desire to teach Black and Brown students. There may be times you feel like the teacher is targeting you. While attending various meetings and conferences, principals have shared encounters they've had with teachers who brashly informed them they did not want to teach "those" students. Imagine how those students were being treated. How sad.

Nevertheless, students, it is vital to not be negligent of your responsibilities to avoid giving any reasons to be removed from class. Simply stated, a student's responsibility includes reporting to class on time, being respectful, completing all assignments, and then transitioning to the next class. These recommendations, along with informing parents, are the most impactful suggestions I can convey to those who feel they are being treated unfairly.

It is crucial for students to remember that it does not matter if you like your teacher or if they adore you. However, it is nonnegotiable that you are treated fairly. Do not aggravate the situation because the teacher will most likely have the last say. I often reiterated to my students that their misconduct will not modify the status of the teacher's employment but how students respond can change their existing educational status and possibly expose students to disciplinary actions. Therefore, it would behoove students to avoid misconduct in the first place and immediately ask for assistance if trouble is lurking.

Make no mistake, the teacher is the authority figure in his or her classroom and students are required to abide by his or her classroom rules. However, there are times when students may feel unsupported and are unsure of how to handle the matter, particularly our minority students. During my tenure as an administrator, many students asked me questions such as, "What should I do if I feel my teacher or a peer is treating me unfairly during class and the teacher won't allow me to leave and report it?" Whereas, some may believe the answer is as simple as, "Just deal with it." Unfortunately, it is certainly not that simplistic. I have witnessed situations escalate to where a student gets into a great deal of trouble because they were not allowed to remove themselves from volatile situations. However, if a student had been given permission to leave during such erratic times, most of the circumstances could have been avoided or resolved instantaneously. Therefore, if students find themselves in this particular scenario, I highly recommend this suggestion:

1. Initially, make every attempt to sit quietly but when prompted with a question, respond without delay and as precisely as possible. If the situation escalates or you feel the environment is too toxic for you to remain there, make a request to report to the office. It is the best practice, and the classroom rule, to get permission before leaving. Nevertheless, if after several denied requests, an option would be to respectfully inform the teacher you are going directly to the office, letting him/her know it is imperative you speak with an administrator immediately. Prior to leaving, compose a list of students who sit in close proximity to you. They can potentially serve as witnesses for you later if needed.

2. It is essential to go directly to the office, absolutely no detours. Once at the office, ask for an administrator and call your

parents. Be sure to share in detail what occurred along with your notes and witnesses.

Parents, of course, a follow-up is highly advised in a situation like this. I suggest utilizing the following process:

1. Request a meeting with the administration and inform them you would also like to have a conference with the teacher involved in this situation. Most likely, your request to meet with the teacher will not be granted the very same day because the teacher's schedule has to be taken into consideration and because of their contractual rights. Yet, you can expect a meeting to take place within the next day or two.

2. Parents, upon completion of the conference with the teacher and administration, you will have a few choices to ponder based on the information you received. One of your choices may be to request a deeper investigation into the classroom issue, or you may want to consider moving your student from the class. Although your student has a right to remain there if they have not done anything egregious, you may still want to consider transferring them to a different class for their comfort. Of course, this may depend on how much time remains before the end of the semester and/or if your child wants to remain there. Do not assume the student will automatically request to be removed from a situation of this sort. I have been surprised that students will sometimes refuse to leave a classroom where they do not feel sup-

ported and there are countless reasons why. For example, the student may not want their daily class schedule to be altered because oftentimes, changing one class can result in a huge shuffle of all the other courses. If the student elects to remain in the class, it is going to require parents to monitor the situation regularly. Parents, you may monitor this situation in a number of ways, but I suggest daily conversations with your student as well as directly communicating with the teacher via e-mail or phone calls.

THE ALTERNATIVE LEARNING CENTER (ALC)

Parents, if your student is being referred to an alternative school, I highly recommend you gather as much information as possible before accepting the recommendation unless you have unequivocal proof your student's actions rose to the level to warrant those consequences. Even so, the following is suggested prior to accepting the relocation:

1. Ask your student to provide you with verbatim details that led to the situation.
2. Request to review your student's statement if you were not present when it was written.
3. Request to see all evidence related to the infraction such as videos. You will not be shown another student's and/or, perhaps, teacher's statements. However, the administration can share what they were told by those who made statements, although their names will most likely be kept anonymous. Often, the teacher will freely share information that pertains to the circumstances. Be sure to ask specific

questions, for example: "What evidence is there that my student committed the infraction?" Note: Remember, an SRO (School Resource Officer) is not held to the same parent requests as the administration, particularly if the incident becomes a police matter.

4. If your student is emphatic about not committing the infraction, immediately request a meeting with the principal. You may be told the principal is not available. If you are adamant and insist, usually the principal will meet with you or appoint the second in command to do so right away. If this fails, request to schedule an appointment. The immediate follow-up meeting with the principal may not be applicable if your student committed an egregious offense, e.g., caused severe physical harm to another, brought a weapon to school, or made direct threats. If any of the aforementioned are involved, the primary focus shifts to ensuring that everyone involved is safe. Removing your student from the educational environment at that time is paramount so that he or she does not harm anyone or themselves.

5. Once again, if your student is adamant about not breaking the school rules, there is no concrete evidence, and you are not able to get clarification at the school level, ask to speak with the area superintendent or a district level employee. Still, if you are unsatisfied with the outcome of the meeting with the area superintendent, request to meet with the district superintendent. Hopefully, before you have gotten to this point, a resolution is reached to your satisfaction. Be steadfast in your desires to

resolve the issue. It is unlikely your student will be transferred or recommended for an alternative school at this point if no concrete evidence is provided. If it is verified your child committed an offense rising to the level of being referred to the alternative school, you should be sure to attend the school-based administrative hearing. During the hearing, be sure to see and hear all details including information from the counselor, teachers, and all discipline data. If the final decision is to move forward with the alternative school placement, and you still have doubts, you have every right to request a district-level hearing before the school board. At the district hearing, the meeting will most likely include school board members, the school's principal or designee, the assistant principal of discipline, and perhaps the SRO and witnesses or other staff who could clarify the event.

6. If there is an abundance of evidence supporting the recommendation for placement at the ALC, there are still other options available for your student. For example, if you are in a position to ensure monitoring of virtual or home schooling, you may consider those options. Though selecting not to utilize the ALC as the new placement can be risky, as your child could fall behind or have to start courses over. Just be cognizant that there are other options in lieu of going to the ALC. I highly recommend visiting the alternative center prior to making your final decision. When the ALC is organized properly, they provide a means for students to receive a solid education with the least amount of disruption to their pedagogical routines. Please note that I am not advo-

cating against ALCs if your student's offense reaches the level to warrant the recommendation. However, it is advantageous for your student that all alternatives are considered.

DO NOT ALLOW A SUSPENSION TO HINDER ACADEMIC PROGRESS

If your student is referred to an in-school suspension (ISS), I recommend the following:

1. It is imperative your student reports to ISS on the date assigned. If not, the student will most likely be suspended from school. Avoid out-of-school suspensions because when your student misses school, it is easy for him or her to fall behind in his or her courses, leading to further disciplinary issues as a result of frustrations.
2. If your student is suspended from school, please do not allow being at home to become a comfortable and pleasant experience. Throughout my years in education, students have shared with me that being at home is not a punishment. I recommend you put them on a rigorous schedule during out-of-school suspension time. Be sure to request all their makeup work from teachers immediately. Although you may not be at home during the day to supervise, arrange a study and work schedule for them. Be specific to include an hour-by-hour time on school assignments. I recommend, if your student does not comply, be prepared to provide consequences. Examples of consequences would be to take away cell phone privileges, restrict television time and social

gatherings, or whatever you feel will force your student to reflect on his or her actions. I recommend the above restrictions based on information my students shared with me as intolerable.

3. Once your student transitions back into school, reach out to the teachers and follow up on his or her behavior and coursework on a regular basis. Be open to sharing various means of your contact information such as your cell phone, home number, spouse and grandparents' contact information. It is imperative the school is able to reach you if needed. When I was a principal, too often, I heard how difficult it was to reach certain parents. I was well aware of who and what they were referring to and therefore, at every opportunity, I reminded parents to leave contact information.

AVOID CONFLICTS WITH THE SCHOOL RESOURCE OFFICER

Over the last few decades, School Resource Officers (SRO) have become more visible on school campuses. An SRO is primarily responsible for providing extra security and ensuring safety for students, faculty, and staff. An SRO plays a substantial role in maintaining order on the campus. I continuously implored my students to never allow an infraction to escalate to it becoming a police matter because, in all actuality, SROs are police officers who are assigned to work at the schools.

A significant aspect of discipline parents and students need to be cognizant of is that once the police take over a situation on school grounds, the administration is required to abstain from interfering. The principal may want to oppose a student being arrested for a school offense or disturbance; however, if the officer on duty deems the offense to be a police matter, the principal's input may be irrelevant. Hence, this is one reason it is vitally important for students not to allow infractions to elevate to where the police are involved. As principal, I never requested or instructed an SRO to press charges against any of my students. This includes when I was taken to the hospital because of an injury incurred while trying to stop a physical altercation between two large males. I categorically understood the students were not deliberately trying to harm me; I was a solid object in their path to pursue each other.

HOW YOU SHOULD RESPOND IF AN SRO IS SUMMONED TO YOUR CLASS FOR YOUR MISCONDUCT

There are times when School Resource Officers (SRO) are summoned to the classroom to assist with misconduct. The following is a list of strategies to aid students in ensuring they do NOT allow an SRO-involved incident to escalate. Students must indisputably avoid putting themselves into a position leading to an arrest.

If the SRO asks a student to leave a classroom with him/her, the student should do so quietly and without hesitation. Even if the infraction does not warrant the involvement of the SRO, the student should still adhere to the following:

1. Follow directions to leave the classroom or you may be written up for insubordination or worse. Additionally, more substantial consequences could be issued by the SRO.

2. If you have not committed an egregious or dangerous offense, most likely, the SRO will refrain from managing the situation and defer it to an administrator. At that point, do not forget to respectfully request your parents are called. This is to minimize your chances of receiving excessive infractions and to provide an extra layer of support. Please, remember the police are not held to the same restrictions as administrators and therefore, they may or may not allow you to reach out to your parents right away, depending on the severity of the situation.

3. Remember, your ultimate goal is to avoid being arrested, and to return to your class as expeditiously as possible. All things being fair and equitable, adhering to the request of the authorities with limited outburst is the swiftest way to return to your regular setting.

"Education is that whole system of human training within and without the school house walls, which molds and develops men."

– W.E.B. DuBois

CHAPTER 5

Mentoring Programs Provide Extra Layers of Support

When I was a pre-teen and a teenager, I vividly recall observing successful adults in their personal or professional environments and pondered ways to emulate them. When I reflect now, I realize I was unofficially adopting a mentor or role model for myself by mere observation. Throughout my adolescence, I found myself intrigued by adults. I carefully observed their actions, the way in which they presented themselves, and how they responded to me and others.

I was impressionable, and therefore, indelible imprints were chiseled into my memory as I worked silently to embrace characteristics of adults I encountered. These observations comforted me as I transitioned from a child into a young adult. Admittedly, as a youth, I had no clear understanding of what a mentor was, and I do not believe the term mentor was utilized nearly as frequently as it is now. Nevertheless, embracing mentorship and role models was another significant turning point in my life.

Once I began my career as a teacher, I was fortunate enough to have a mentor who encouraged me. I valued her input, and as a result, promised I would give back by serving as a mentor to others, perhaps establishing mentoring programs one day. The commitment to myself to give back what was given to me came to fruition when I was able to create a mentoring program at the high school where I worked, but the greatest impact emanated once I transferred out of the classroom into a leadership position.

Further, because there was such a small number of individuals of color serving in leadership roles in my school district, I felt inclined to advance myself professionally to become an educational leader. By doing so, it further expanded my platform to serve as a mentor and to encourage other adults to become mentors as well. Additionally, it was important to me for my own children and other students of color to see people who looked like them in more leadership roles within the school system. Hence, I asked myself, why not me? Therefore, when the assistant principal of discipline position became available at a middle school, I understood the importance of securing that position.

Even with my commitment to move forward, the transition from the classroom to becoming an administrator was not an easy one because teaching had brought me inordinate joy. To see the proverbial light bulb illuminate in a student's face when they finally grasp a concept was priceless. Nevertheless, after careful consideration, I accepted the position as assistant principal of discipline at the local middle school just a few miles from the high school where I taught on the Space Coast near central Florida.

Since the duration of my career was spent teaching at the high school level, I was accustomed to students behaving in a mature manner. In addition, my classroom was structured in such a way that my students were abreast of my expectations and the high standards I set for them. Therefore, I experienced little to no classroom discipline issues. Yet, I was well aware there were concerns with discipline in other areas of the high school. I share this because once I began my position as the assistant principal in charge of discipline at the middle school, I was oblivious to the extreme discipline issues awaiting me there. Of course, I was fully aware discipline was a concern because middle school students are at an awkward age where many of them are on a roller coaster with their emotions and hormones. Although I had completed my research prior to accepting the position, I was unaware of the extent of discipline problems.

Before the end of the first two weeks of the school year, I had observed a large majority of the students sent to my office for discipline issues were students of color. Actually, there were more Black students sent to my office than any other race. The office was continuously overflowing with students. I immediately recognized I needed to swiftly develop a plan to curtail the vast number of daily discipline referrals. My goals were to limit the number of students missing valuable instructional time, minimize transfers to alternative schools, and decrease the dropout rate.

Therefore, I met with the principal and expressed my desire to create and implement a mentoring program. I expressed to him that research showed students who had extra layers of support had fewer discipline issues, performed better academically, and were less likely to dropout. I stressed to him the program would be specifically designed to provide an extra layer of educational and emotional support for underserved students. The principal embraced my proposal to initiate the mentoring program and commended me for doing so.

After the meeting, I next shared the information with a colleague. She appeared to show enthusiasm for the program and agreed it would make a significant difference. Behind the scenes, I continued tweaking the details. However, I found that throughout the day, the number of students with disciplinary issues was overwhelming and did not provide sufficient time for me to rollout the program. Quite frankly, I was so overwhelmed and found it incredulous so many discipline problems existed, which required me to work extended hours. I would remain at work late into the evenings to stay current on the vast number of phone calls and the insurmountable amount of paperwork. My work carried over into my home life because of the sheer volume, and therefore, once home, I continued to work late into the evenings.

As each day passed, I found I was so inundated with a constant flow of discipline referrals, I became incredibly fatigued and could not break away to find time to officially begin the program. Then one day, in the midst of the chaos of the office traffic, my aforementioned colleague contacted me and said, "I know you are always busy with discipline

referrals, but if you rollout the mentoring program, it will probably help." I wanted so
desperately to initiate the program, but at this
point, I was so inundated with responding to
student misconduct matters, I rarely found
time to handle other matters. However, after
discussing this further with my colleague, I
knew she was right. I was now inclined to
accept her urging me to move forward. If I were
going to provide that extra layer of support for
the students, I had to implement the program
expeditiously. I reflected, re-evaluated my
schedule, and mustered up the energy to set a
start date.

I utilized data such as discipline, academic
and attendance records to select the students
for the program. Teacher recommendations
were also an integral part of the selection
process. Once I had compiled a list of the
students who revealed signs of needing the
most support, I forwarded a detailed e-mail to
the teachers to get their buy-in. Amazingly, the
program particulars and the targeted students
were well received by the teachers. Many
teachers signed on immediately to become
mentors. Because I had such a large number of
students needing extra support, some teachers
accepted more than one mentee. I also solicited
support from community members to serve as
mentors and they welcomed the opportunity to
invest in the lives of our students.

Initially, I did not have a coordinator for the
program and therefore, the responsibilities were
left solely to me and a volunteer to ensure the
program operated smoothly. Although the
program was welcomed by the faculty and staff,
the process was not without obstacles, but
through our determined efforts to assist the
students, we were able to get activated with

minimal issues. It was amazing to see how receptive and elated most of the students were to know that they had a mentor on campus. The basic program requirements were as follows:

1. The mentors and mentees must commit to meeting no less than once a week.
2. Parents and guardians agree to allow mentors to have access to a mentee's grades and discipline records.
3. Mentees agree to attend help sessions if grades are in jeopardy.
4. Teachers are encouraged to mentor students who are in their class, as well as those who are not in their class.
5. Mentors are encouraged to attend special events of mentees.
6. Mentors and mentees are encouraged to have lunch together at least once a month.
7. Mentees are encouraged to give back to the community by participating in community events, such as planting a garden and sharing the harvest with others.

I was optimistic about the initial imple-mentation of the mentoring program, its success, and the future support the students would receive. Overall, students, parents, and teachers were receptive, and this removed most trepidations that may have existed. Of course, comparable to most new endeavors, a few of the students were initially apprehensive to be-coming involved with this new program.

There was a young lady in particular I shall never forget. For the purpose of this story, I shall refer to her as Victoria. I was a novice administrator at a new school and therefore, unfamiliar with most of the student body at the time. However, I quickly became acquainted with Victoria because of her habitual misconduct. Victoria was a beautiful girl and quite precocious in her physical development and dressed inappropriately. She skipped school regularly and when she was there, she was disruptive and insubordinate with her teachers, often yelling and swearing at them. Additionally, she often got into verbal and near physical altercations with her peers. Victoria had no respect for adult authority nor herself. Victoria's behavior was growing more destructive with the passing of each day.

My own two children were school-age during that time. My daughter, Jada, was a freshman in high school and my son, Marcus, was in middle school. As a matter of fact, Marcus attended the same middle school during my time there as assistant principal. Perhaps it was my motherly intuition, but I felt a deep desire to take Victoria on personally as my mentee. I approached Victoria, provided her details about the mentoring program, informing her I wanted to be her mentor. To my dismay and without any hesitation, Victoria adamantly expressed her resistance to getting into the mentoring program. I would not accept her refusal, as I had reviewed her data and background, finding she was a perfect candidate for the program.

During my examination of her background, I learned Victoria had a troubled home life where very few rules were enforced. Further, during one of Victoria's visits to the office for discipline issues, she blurted out with tears streaming down her face that her mother didn't care what she did. I questioned Victoria about her comment, and she elaborated that she was allowed to stay out until 2 or 3 a.m., even on school nights. I pressed her more and dejectedly she shared that she was sexually active with boys and changed partners on a frequent basis. After hearing this information, I contacted Victoria's mother and requested a conference. Later that day, to my surprise, her mother came to the school. With Victoria's permission, I was prepared to discuss what Victoria had shared with me but as soon as her mother entered the room, Victoria said to her mother, "You don't care what I do." She went on to remind her mother of the lack of parental supervision, having no restrictions and other relevant issues. Victoria and her mother both began to cry. Admittedly, we had a deep conversation and before it was all over, Victoria's mother stated that she planned to do better. Clearly, Victoria was not convinced because when her mother left, she told me that nothing would change.

Needless to say, I refused to give up on her becoming my mentee. Eventually, Victoria accepted my offer and ultimately did exceptionally well receiving additional support. Getting to this point was not easy but I was steadfast on successfully mentoring Victoria. We met nearly every day, even if it were for only a few minutes. I made a point to expose Victoria to educational field trips, discussions with prominent leaders, and we would have lunch together on a regular basis. After being in the program for a little while, it became routine for Victoria to locate me for our daily conversations. If for some reason I was delayed because of a meeting or other commitment, Victoria was sure to locate me before the day was over. Pleasingly, she finished the year with enhanced improvements in her attendance and her grades improved tremendously. In addition, Victoria's days of being sent to the assistant principal's office were virtually nonexistent. We continued our mentor/mentee relationship even when she transferred to high school. Victoria completed high school and moved from our small town to a larger city where she found more employment and social opportunities. She is now married with a child and has a reputable job. Victoria is a perfect example of how providing students with an extra layer of support can be the catalyst for positive change.

Under my direction, the mentoring program served more than 300 students from our community. With the substantial support of the amazing coordinator who came on board to assist me, the area superintendent requested we provide training to other principals in the district on how to implement a mentoring program at their schools by sharing the intricate details. The desired outcome was for other schools to consider implementing a similar plan with the hopes of improving academic success and decreasing discipline issues.

My coordinator and I were pleased to learn that several of the mentors expressed their commitment to continue mentoring their mentees as they transitioned to high school. It became normal to see mentors at the extra-curricular events of their mentees. Once specific data was collected and analyzed to evaluate the effectiveness of the program, story after story revealed students benefited significantly. Many of these students have built long-lasting relationships with their mentors.

Faculty and community members took a vested interest in the students which was instrumental in fostering success for the students. Undoubtably, mentors are able to provide an extra layer of support, academically and emotionally. I can attest firsthand to how mentoring programs are particularly important for underserved and underprivileged students. Furthermore, even if students come from a home with parents who are visibly involved in every aspect of their daily lives, mentors are able to provide additional support for students of all backgrounds, no matter their circumstances. Therefore, it is without any hesitation I recommend educators to implement more mentoring programs and for families to take full advantage of the opportunity to participate if it is offered.

"The beautiful thing about learning is that no one can take it away from you."

-B.B. King

CHAPTER 6

TESTING, TESTING, TESTING:
The Concordant Score
to the Rescue

Concordant Score: Refers to establishing a relationship between scores on assessments that measure similar constructs. (act.org)

Under my leadership, my school used concordant scores to enhance graduation opportunities when a student struggled with passing the state assessment. In laymen's terms, concordant scores may be substituted for a state required assessment if the score meets the minimum requirements set forth by the state. Concordant scores provide students with multiple testing opportunities to meet graduation requirements.

An example of how a concordant score could benefit a student is if the student is unable to successfully pass the reading section of the state assessment, but his or her scores on the reading portion of the SAT or ACT are within an acceptable range, those scores could be substituted for the state assessment in the category of reading. Using the concordant score provides students with multiple opportunities to earn a proficient or higher score on another construct test rather than relying solely on the state assessment. Unfortunately, many of our Black and Brown students struggle with passing the state assessment and therefore, the concordant score is a great opportunity to enhance their chances for success.

During my interview for the position of principal of the high school, I shared with the interview panel a list of what I wanted to accomplish during my first year on the job. My list was not extensive, as it is common knowledge in the education arena that, in most instances, one's first year should mainly serve as an observational year. Therefore, I had no intentions of making many significant changes. My list contained modest goals. However, one goal I felt strongly about was reviewing and analyzing data in an effort to uncover ways to improve the graduation rate. Once hired and after reviewing the data, I found areas I wanted to explore further. I was certain I could provide strategies to enhance the graduation percentile.

Prior to becoming the principal, my high school administrative experience was limited to a short stint as the temporary replacement assistant principal of discipline for an administrator who was on leave. Hence, I did not have an elaborate educational plan documented, with the exception of eventually implementing the extensive training I had received on standards-based instructions. Of course, my priority was to provide students with as much collective and individualized support as possible. However, my plan soon became more deliberate when I uncovered a testing opportunity for my students that needed to be amplified.

Although I had previously taught at the high school level for approximately twenty years, there had been no pressing reason for me to maintain regular or direct communication with the guidance department or testing coordinators during the time I served as a teacher. Yet, almost instantaneously upon becoming the high school principal, I immediately positioned myself to understand intricate details of the testing process. Once I became acclimated with the high school testing process, I then discovered there was a cohort of students who had made multiple unsuccessful attempts to pass the state assessment. Upon deeper analysis, I realized an overwhelming number of them were students of color and many of them were enrolled in the eleventh or twelfth grades. This alerted me to the fact that they had few opportunities to master the necessary skills to pass the state assessment or face not graduating on time. In fact, a few of the seniors only had one more such opportunity prior to the graduation ceremony. As you can imagine, some of those students expressed feelings of desperation and had low morale about the prospect of not finishing with their class.

After examining this further, I found that many schools were maximizing opportunities to use the concordant score process to their advantage and as a result, had fewer students in this ineffective category. Discovering this motivated me to work even harder to provide my students with as many testing opportunities as possible.

Therefore, students who had attempted to pass the tests multiple times were identified and targeted for interventions. I, along with another team member, personally contacted each parent for a phone conference to discuss the details of their students' testing circumstances. During the conversations with the parents, we explained exactly what a concordant score was and the specific options their students had moving forward. Emphasis was placed on how critical it was for their student to utilize the concordant scores to their advantage as a replacement for the state assessment. I was pleasantly surprised when the parents expressed gratification for the call which revealed options for their students. Some of the parents, particularly my minority parents, stated they were unaware of the process but were elated to learn this new information. Although the parents strongly supported their student moving forward with additional testing, some acknowledged they did not have the financial resources to pay for the tests. Under no circumstances did I want the lack of funds to be a deterrent for the students seizing this opportunity. Therefore, I was compelled to reallocate funds in my school-based budget to cover the expense of the tests. By doing so, it eliminated a possible obstacle and prevented parents from having to incur the costs or deny their student an opportunity.

Further, once I had a commitment from the students and their parents, I met with team members to strategize an individual remedial study plan for each student. This plan required students to practice regularly using an electronic program called Khan Academy which allows students to hone in on the areas where they need the most practice. Students would also draw on other educational resources to support their learning goals. The outcome of the team's effort was positive and as each of the testing results were published, brief, individual celebrations ensued for all students who were able to score high enough to use the concordant score in place of the state assessment.

Facilitating this testing process brought me pleasure for several reasons. The main reason was that it removed what had appeared to be an impassable obstacle standing between my students and their pending graduation. Seniors in particular, many of whom had been trying to pass the state assessment for a couple of years had almost given up hope, now expressed authentic joy and eagerly anticipated the walk across the stage with their diplomas in-hand.

Additionally, maximizing the use of the concordant scores as well as other strategies increased the graduation rate by more than five percent by the end of the second year of my leadership. Even if only one student had graduated as a result of the measures and interventions my team and I implemented, I would have been content. Having numerous students meet this goal brought me considerable joy. Some of the students actually shed tears when they realized that they would be able to remain with their graduating cohorts. I vividly recall one young man in particular who shared with me that at times he was embarrassed because he was a senior and had not passed the test. As a result, he attended some of the intervening help sessions and insisted that he was diligently working on the Khan Academy program at home on a consistent basis. He further shared he felt the interventions were helping him and he was correct. Upon learning that he had passed the last test offered before graduation, he gave me a huge hug while barely keeping the tears from streaming down his face. His parents had expressed to me that he had almost given up hope and that they were so grateful that we had encouraged him to keep trying. As he walked across the stage on graduation night, it was me who could barely contain my tears. I thought to myself, this student was obstinate in his pursuit to avoid dropping out of school after repeatedly failing the state assessments.

Another emotionally charged story related to passing a concordant score was two girls who had a very close friendship. Although they had both struggled with passing the state assessments, one passed early during her senior year and they celebrated, but when I looked deep into the eyes of the one who had not passed, I could see that she was embarrassed and frightened. Later, she confirmed my intuition and stated that she was deeply afraid of being left behind. I encouraged her to continue attending the help sessions preparing her to pass the concordant test. She did. She passed the test on the very last opportunity, prior to the graduation ceremony. She walked across the stage and afterward, she and her best friend celebrated each other. There were many poignant stories of my students being able to graduate with the use of the concordant score and it pleases me that they were able to seize the opportunity.

It is paramount for students and parents to know about the state's process of allowing a concordant or aggregate score to be used as a replacement for the state assessments. Interventions and additional testing opportunities can make the difference between a student graduating, being retained, or dropping out of school altogether. Successful interventions subsequently serve as platforms to support students who wanted to attend post-secondary institutions or move into gainful employment.

SUMMER SCHOOL

Summer school is another resource students should consider if they need additional academic help or if deficiencies are revealed. Obviously, most students do not favor summer school because it is an extension of the school year. Sometimes students can fall behind with their credits for various reasons; however, it should not automatically mean the student will not be able to graduate on time. If students take advantage of repeating a course through summer school, they are provided with this viable option to stay on track. Because summer school is not popular with students, it is sometimes not used by those students who need it the most. In order to avoid this issue, I highly recommend that prior to the beginning of each school year, parents and students plan a meeting with the guidance counselor to review credits, schedules, testing data, placement options, and other pertinent information.

CREDIT RETRIEVAL

Finally, another way for students to make up failed courses is through credit retrieval. Credit retrieval entails taking an online course in a subject a student did not take or failed. Usually, the student will take the course in place of an elective course. While giving up an elective course is not popular, credit retrieval is a viable option for students to help ensure they graduate on time. Each school has its own unique structure of credit retrieval, and that structure deserves widespread support. It is, after all, the responsibility of the village to ensure our students have every possible opportunity for success within reach.

"Upon the subject of education, not presuming to dictate any plan or system respecting it, I can only say that I view it as the most important subject which we as a people can be engaged in."

Abraham Lincoln

CHAPTER 7

Exceptional Student Education and the Minority Student

E xceptional Student Education (ESE), refers to children who are gifted and those with disabilities who need specially designed instruction and related services. (fldoe.org) ESE is a distinct area in education minority parents of students with disabilities should pay particular attention to if the student qualifies for these services. The federal and state government requires specific and deliberate attention be given to this area of education to ensure all ESE students are treated fairly. Additionally, their Individual Educational Plans (IEP), or other related plans, must be current and designed specifically for each student. ESE students must be afforded access to a free and appropriate education with emphasis placed on their particular and specific needs.

While serving as principal, I was steadfast in assuring my ESE team provided accurate information when developing Individual Educational Plans for qualified students. I took every aspect of my job seriously and attended as many ESE meetings as possible. However, I intentionally focused particular attention on my ESE population for several reasons. The primary reason was the importance of ensuring my students had a voice and their needs were met accordingly. I found this population of students benefited and excelled when their accommodations or modifications were being utilized properly, and conversely, when students were not provided adequate services or declined their rights to use their ESE services, they struggled unnecessarily and sometimes significantly.

Identifying and determining if a child will benefit from ESE services by testing or some sort of evaluation is the first step. The next crucial step is to attend the meeting where the Individual Educational Plan is established. The meeting is extremely important, and it is highly advised for parents to do their research prior to attending an IEP meeting to ensure the student's needs are being addressed sufficiently. During the meeting, the team will make recommendations for accommodations or modifications tailored to the specific needs of the child.

If your child is recommended for ESE testing, ask questions about how s/he was identified for needing this additional support. Although parents must give permission for their child to be tested, some students are identified incorrectly. Far too many minorities are identified as ESE when in fact, stereotyping or other issues may be the real culprit. A family member of mine shared with me early in her son's elementary years, he arrived home with a letter from his teacher stating the teacher felt he needed to be tested for Exceptional Student Education services. My family member was adamant that if her child had met the requirements and could have benefited from those services, then of course she would have accepted the recommendation and approved testing. However, her son had only been in the presence of his teacher for less than eight hours and there were no artifacts or evidence to support this teacher's theory of him meeting the criteria as an ESE candidate, yet she had already decided the young Black male had a learning disability.

Upon speaking with the teacher, the only explanation received for the referral for ESE testing was that the child did not seem focused and perhaps hyper. Admittedly, the child was a tad bit hyper, however, that did not hinder his ability to absorb, analyze, interpret, and grasp instructional content, and rather quickly I might add.

Therefore, his parent declined to have him ESE tested at that time. Perhaps if the teacher had spent more time observing him and/or charting his behavior, the parent would have taken the recommendation. However, there is an awareness of stigmas being so easily affixed to Black and Brown children, stigmas having nothing to do with their cognitive abilities, and my family member was not going to allow that label to be unnecessarily attached to her son. Additionally, these erroneous labels have been viewed as a pipeline to prisons for our Black and Brown students, particularly our males. This mother was committed to providing her son with the resources and support needed for him to be college ready and thankfully, her son recently graduated from college and was a member of the honor society while attending.

Although some parents may decline to allow their child to be tested for ESE, please understand that if needed, ESE supports are beneficial to students. Those services should never be declined if indeed the student can benefit from additional academic or other supports. However, under no circumstances should a child be identified as having a cognitive learning disability for ordinary misconduct, attendance, or any other reasons unrelated to their ability to learn and absorb the information.

Further, in planning for a child to receive educational support services, it is important for parents to know the difference between an accommodation or a modification. Accommodations change *how* a child learns. Modifications change *what* a child is taught or is expected to learn.

To provide further clarification, examples of how modifications and accommodations are used to support student learning include, but are not limited to, the following:

Accommodations:
- A student with poor eyesight may be allowed to utilize a device to assist with reading passages (i.e., voice recognition or text-to-speech).
- Students are allowed to take tests in different settings, away from the whole group.
- A student may be provided additional time to take a test.

Modifications:

- A test is modified (changed) for a student based on their learning needs.
- If a student struggles with reading, they may be allowed to read only part of a book.
- Students being allowed to outline instead of writing an entire essay.

Another important plan for Black and Brown families to become familiar with is a 504 plan. The 504 plans are a result of Section 504 of the US Rehabilitation Act of 1973, designed to help parents of students with physical or mental impairments in schools. These plans legally ensure students will be treated fairly. Students qualify for 504 plans if they have physical or mental impairments affecting or limiting any of their abilities to:

- Walk, breathe, eat, or sleep
- Communicate, see, hear, or speak
- Read, concentrate, think, or learn
- Stand, bend, lift, or work

kidshealth.org

A 504 plan helps alleviate learning barriers that make it more difficult for students to comprehend. Parents may request an evaluation for a 504 for their students if they suspect there is a learning barrier. In most cases, students are tested after they have had a medical diagnosis, but this is not the only avenue to getting the tests.

To provide further clarification, examples of how 504s are used to support student learning include, but are not limited to, the following:

1. Extra test time (most common)
2. Location of the test
3. Verbal testing
4. Social/emotional support
5. Reduced homework
6. Preferential seating

There are many more examples of how 504 plans can be utilized to support a student. However, far too often, our Black and Brown students may qualify for additional supports but may forgo testing. Sometimes, once identified, they underutilize these services whereas from my experiences, the large majority of their counterparts not only use the supports, but many know verbatim what the accommodations or modifications are. Students should be well versed on the contents of their 504 plans or IEPs and utilize their modifications and accommodations accordingly.

Those who work in the field of education, or those who are familiar with the ESE, understand that districts and schools receive increased funding for students classified as ESE. If children are identified and evaluated accurately, each school must provide the services the student deserves.

The following is a summary of suggestions I recommend for students and parents if the student qualifies for evaluation and/or receives ESE services:

1. Be an active participant. Although parents are required to be included in the meetings, please be sure you, the parent or guardian, have a clear understanding of what services are written in the IEP for your student before leaving said meeting. The plan is

usually designed by a team consisting of the parents, ESE specialist, guidance counselor, ESE case manager, LEA which is a Location Education Agent. The LEA's role is to ensure the district is complying with all requirements.

2. Require the case manager or designee to explain each component in detail with you and your student.

3. Set up a system whereby you are checking to ensure that your student is utilizing the accommodations or modifications designed for them. Too often, I was told by a teacher a student said s/he didn't need or want extra test time. If extended time is included in their education plan, they should utilize the extra time. It can be quite advantageous for students to do so.

4. Finally, telephone, e-mail, or conference at least once each quarter with your student's case manager and request your student's IEP, or other relevant plans, are reviewed according to the guidelines or sooner if deemed necessary.

If your student is identified as ESE, your child should continue to be held to high standards within the realm of their disability. It is imperative for students to be pushed and challenged to ensure they reach their fullest potential. Their abilities, and NOT their limitations, should be emphasized.

For parents who may feel their student may have some educational struggles outside of the ordinary or needs additional educational support and you are not sure if they have a learning disability, you have every right to request your student be evaluated. Testing is done at absolutely no cost to you but when done properly, can provide you with information to help your student be successful and minimize his or her frustrations.

One of the things that frustrated me were the various stories shared about observations of ESE students in their learning environment. For example, a colleague shared with me when she visited a classroom, an ESE student had his head down on the desk sleeping. When the teacher was asked why the student was sleeping, the teacher responded, "She doesn't feel like working today," or "I didn't want to upset him by waking him." These types of responses are offensive to hear and set low expectations for the student. Reasons like this, allowing a student to become a non-participant in their educational process, are unacceptable. Even if a student is upset because he or she is not permitted to sleep in class, there are definite ways to handle such situations by reaching out for additional support from the administrative team or guidance counselors, and of course, the parents. We cannot allow our Black and Brown students to be held to lower expectations than their non-Black or Brown peers by their teachers simply because they are quiet.

I was intrigued to speak with professionals who have worked within the ESE field for extended periods of time. Therefore, I interviewed two ESE persons who have worked extensively in this area.

INTERVIEWEE #1

JANA STOKES, ESE ADVOCATE AND FOUNDER OF RYAN'S GIFT OF ADVOCACY

Jana is the mother of a special needs child and uses her voice to fight for the rights of students with learning disabilities or those who are financially underprivileged. Jana actually began her advocacy for ESE students because her own child was not receiving sufficient ESE support. As a result, she learned as much as possible about the laws of ESE and became well versed with Individuals with the Disabilities Education Act (IDEA). In addition, she has worked diligently to expand her knowledge as it relates to FAPE, which stands for Free Appropriate Public Education and falls under Section 504.

Note:

IDEA is the nation's federal special education law that ensures public schools serve the educational needs of students with disabilities. (ncld.org)

The Section 504 regulation requires a school district to provide a 'free appropriate public education' (FAPE) to each qualified person with a disability who is in the school district's jurisdiction, regardless of the nature or severity of the person's disability. (ed.gov)

Because of Jana's personal and professional experiences in the ESE arena, I felt compelled to share her suggestions. Jana makes the following recommendations for parents as it relates to ensuring their children's needs are met:

1. Be proactive rather than re-active. Jana indicated that she does not often receive calls from parents soliciting her support as an advocate until their student is experiencing problems with the lack of sup-

port, ultimately making her job of advocating for them much more difficult. She is a staunch believer in one should never attend an IEP meeting without the representation of an ESE advocate.

2. Jana believes about 25 percent of the cases she accepts, the school personnel does not know all the facts in order to make the best decision for the student. Further, she believes continuous and more frequent training should take place for administrators, teachers, occupational therapists, physical therapists, directors, and all who are involved in the decision-making process for special education students. Having an advocate present signifies you have someone on your team.

3. Jana highly recommends that parents reach out to an advocate immediately upon their student being diagnosed with a disability. It is then the advocate's job to ensure the student is placed in the least restrictive environment. Additionally, the advocate is responsible for providing clarity to the parents and the students. Parents sometimes feel uncomfortable in these meetings and therefore, as their advocate, she leads the conversations on their behalf.

4. IEPs are never final and should always be updated and/or amended regularly.

5. Jana advises students to utilize their accommodations for their disability to their advantage. For example, if the IEP states the student cannot be marked tardy, then be sure they are not recorded as tardy in the student's attendance record. Additionally, if a student is allotted extended time for assignments, it is to the student's advantage to use the extra time.

6. Jana highly recommends that parents know their student's educational goals prior to attending the IEP meeting. During the meetings, visuals should be provided for parents to follow along with the plan suggested for their student. The reason the meeting goals should be on a projector is because at the end of the meeting, parents are expected to provide a signature to show agreement but having it on the projector, you are able to review the plan as it is presented.

7. Parents must understand that all participants of the meeting should agree on the goals and the goals should be documented.

8. Jana strongly believes each meeting should be recorded for future reference.

9. A caseworker is the school-based employee who is responsible for ensuring that students' accommodations or modifications are accessible. Jana recommends that parents are aware the case manager is a primary contact and the first point of contact for any questions.

10. Once a student is ready to transition from the current ESE setting, advocates work to ensure a smooth transition. Advocates also work to make sure parents and students receive all the information and benefits the student deserves. This includes skills necessary for post-secondary transitions.

Jana states that she truly has a passion for working as an advocate for ESE students and to serve and support our underprivileged students.

INTERVIEWEE #2

RUTH GARY, ESE TEACHER (RETIRED)

Ruth worked as an Exceptional Student Education teacher for 38 years, with the majority of that time spent in the state of Florida. She shared the following information in hopes of helping ESE students and parents understand how to best utilize the services. Ruth believes that oftentimes parents blame themselves if their student has difficulty learning and/or following one-step commands. She emphasizes it is not a reflection of parenting skills if a student needs additional assistance. Although some of the parents she encountered felt their parenting skills were being questioned, and others felt embarrassed to know their student needed intellectual support, she wants parents to understand it is to their student's advantage to maximize ESE services.

Ruth shared the following story about one of her students:

A third-grade Hispanic student in Ruth's class displayed signs of extreme struggle and difficulty with reading. English was not her first language, which further compounded the issue. Additionally, Ruth discovered the student and her family were homeless. When she noticed profound gaps when grading the student's papers, Ruth spoke with the parents about testing and ESE services, but the parents refused. Ruth was convinced the parents re-fused services because they were too proud to admit their student needed assistance, and they were afraid their student's need for assistance was a poor reflection on their parenting skills. Although it saddened Ruth greatly to see the student struggle unnecessarily, she found some solace in knowing the student was able to perform at a level where it placed her in a position to be promoted to the next grade level. However, because the student's grades were consistently low, Ruth was convinced if the student had received ESE support services, she would have been able to be much more successful without barriers.

Ruth emphasizes it is not a stigma for a child to need additional educational supports and suggest the following if your student does need support:

1. Attend ESE meetings to provide input.
2. Ensure the plans are reviewed regularly.
3. Keep up with the homework and communicate with your student's teachers.
4. If students qualify for services, be aware they are entitled to all accommodations and 504 modifications.
5. Just as a parent would take a student to the medical doctor, they should view the ESE specialist in the same light if they suspect the student would benefit from these services.

On the other hand, Ruth felt it important to share that during her tenure, she also found that some students were being referred for ESE services by their teacher when they should not have been. These students were able to perform effectively without the interventions. She further shared that some teachers were surprised once test results returned and revealed the students were performing at or above proficiency without additional support. In cases such as these, Ruth suggests that perhaps the students were not being challenged enough, which may have led the teacher to believe there was a learning disability when, in fact, there was not one. Therefore, it is important to investigate all possibilities as it relates to your student's abilities.

Ruth shares these stories and recommendations with hopes of helping at least one parent and student overcome obstacles and navigate the ESE educational system with a greater awareness. Her mantra is, "I do not believe in a child being labeled as having a learning disability, but instead, that children learn differently."

"Some know the value of education by having it. I know its value by not having it."

Frederick Douglass

CHAPTER 8

The Impact of Virtual Learning on Black and Brown Students:
Having Similarities of the "Summer Slide"

The COVID-19 pandemic has forced millions of us around the world to alter our everyday lives in ways we could have never imagined. We are now forced to think about every move we make. We carefully select which events we will or will not attend and even then, take extreme precautions to maintain our safety. Responsibly, we should wear face masks, avoid large gatherings, wash our hands frequently, and socially distance ourselves as much as possible. Many parents have been forced to work from home and students have been required to participate in distance learning.

Undoubtedly, students across our nation have experienced various degrees of frustrations with virtual learning and, for some, virtual learning was not an anomaly. However, for many of our Black and Brown students, virtual and distance learning was new and required a totally different approach to their customary face-to-face learning styles.

As an educator, I am intrigued to see how this unimaginable pandemic changed the course of how traditional education is now taking place. I knew there would be drastic changes but none of us were prepared for the "new normal."

When the initial announcements of school closures were made, I personally know students who celebrated the announcement. Several parents of school-age students shared that their children were rejoicing. However, as the pandemic required students to remain at home and out of school for an extended period of time, I began to hear stories from parents and friends about how students were starting to exhibit feelings of isolation. Further, some students struggled with grasping the distance learning process and many yearned to be back in the traditional brick and mortar setting.

I received calls from community members and friends asking my professional opinion about the new normal for students as it related to the process and requirements for virtual learning. Parents expressed concerns about their students not retaining enough information to be prepared for the next grade level. Additionally, some revealed their students were experiencing bouts of depression from the lack of social interaction. We have all been greatly affected by the pandemic in various ways, but we must pay close attention to the impact it has on our students.

Contrary to the initial reaction of students who were elated to be out of school, there were many who were saddened by the closures. For example, seniors looked forward to attending school in 2020 and celebrating events associated with graduation in the traditional manner. They had completed every required stage of their education and had reached the finish line. It was difficult to hear some of my relatives and friends express their students' sadness as they realized, although they had worked diligently for twelve years for the ultimate experiences each senior looks forward to, they would not be able to participate in the traditional senior celebratory activities due to the restrictions brought on by the pandemic and social distancing requirements.

As a parent, I experienced the direct impact of virtual educational changes with my son. Thankfully, our situation was not a long-term issue, as he graduated from the University of Central Florida a few months after the pandemic began, with his graduation ceremony being held virtually. Although our family definitely celebrated his accomplishment through the virtual ceremony, like many other families, we had anticipated being in the auditorium screaming his name and afterwards taking memorable photos. He had worked so hard to earn his degree, just as all of his classmates had. Nevertheless, we accepted that although we were not able to celebrate on the actual college campus, we prepared our own home version of the ceremony as did many others across the nation.

It was astonishing to see school closures lasting for such an extended period of time. As I write this book, some schools remain closed and this new normal has become an obvious reality for the many students who yearn to return to campus.

As an educator, I am concerned about how Black and Brown students will fare with the changes school districts face during the pandemic while endeavoring to educate students and maintain high standards. The educational adjustments our students now face have reminded me of something called the "summer slide."

The summer slide is when students don't actively participate in reading or engage in academic learning over the summer and return to school in the fall, displaying a learning gap between those who read and those who did not. It is directly associated with widening of the achievement gap and a hinderance for Black and Brown students showing a decrease in meeting early literacy benchmarks. Unfortunately, the summer slide has been no stranger to students of color and is a culprit for students experiencing some loss of their achievement gains from the previous year. Too often, the minority students return to school and require remediation to mitigate some of the learning gaps resulting over the summer. The summer slide is particularly problematic for students of the lower-socioeconomic background while their counterparts are not impacted nearly as much.

The impact of distance learning on our Black and Brown students, as a result of the pandemic, may resemble the learning gaps similar to those gaps posed by the summer slide theory.

CAUSES OF SUMMER SLIDES

The following information is research-based findings on the summer slide. Some of this information may have a direct correlation to the effects of virtual learning due to the 2020 pandemic:

- *Students in low-income households fall behind an average of two months in reading during the summer. And, summer slide is cumulative, with these learning losses building up each summer.*
- *Summer-learning-loss accounts for two-thirds of the 9th grade achievement gap in reading between students from low-income households and their higher-income peers.*
- *Students from low-income households with access to books over the summer see significantly more gains in reading scores from spring to fall than students from high-income households with access to books and those from low-income households without access to books.*
- *Differences in students' summer learning experiences during their elementary school years can ultimately impact whether they earn a high school diploma and continue to college.*
- *Reading just four to six books over the summer has the potential to prevent a decline in reading achievement scores from the spring to the fall, so even small steps are beneficial.*
- *Preventing summer slide is most effective when community organizations—including schools, public libraries, community centers, parent groups, social service agencies, and others—work together to encourage students to read, make reading fun, and to reach families about the importance of reading over the summer.*

HOW I PREVENTED MY CHILDREN FROM FALLING VICTIM TO THE SUMMER SLIDE

My personal story of combating the summer slide with my own children, who are now college graduates, was when I began giving them books at a young age for birthday and Christmas gifts. I am convinced that by doing this, it fostered their love of books, and hence, both became avid readers. I relished the experiences of taking my children to the library and coaching them as they received their very own library cards.

Additionally, they were so fond of reading, their schedule consisted of visiting the library up to three times per week. I credit their love and frequency of reading to neither of them ever experiencing the summer slide. Quite the contrary, because reading became such an integral part of their day, at one point my son's elementary teacher called to express she had an unusual problem to discuss with me. Initially, I was alarmed because I had never received a disciplinary call. The teacher said she had never had this particular issue occur before and had been teaching for many years. Of course, I wanted her to quickly get to the issue at hand. I was intrigued, concerned, and did not want idle conversation. I soon found out there wasn't a true discipline issue and was actually relieved when she shared that my son was bringing his personal books from home into the classroom. She further shared that she never imagined she would ever have to provide consequences to a student for reading but my son was not paying attention when she delivered group or individual instruction.

Of course, I was not going to consent to her giving my son any substantive consequences for reading. However, I did understand he needed to stay focused on the instructional lessons being presented. Although reading was an amazing way for him to spend his time, I did not want him to fall behind and he needed to follow the teacher's directions. Therefore, my husband and I had what turned out to be a hard conversation with our son, explaining to him, although we were pleased that he loved reading, it was imperative that he leave his books home so he could focus during school.

He did not receive our request well and questioned us because I talked on a regular basis about the importance of reading. He continued to take his books to school despite our conversation and insistence. I was torn because he was not following our instructions; however, we knew if we punished him, we would risk him losing his love for reading, hence, punishment was not an option.

The teacher and I collaborated and reached the agreement that we would check his backpack before he left home and that she would check it when he arrived at school, without giving him any consequences. After numerous attempts, we were finally able to get him to comply with leaving his books at home. One strategy that might have helped was he was allowed to read during activity time, and I kept books in the car so that he could read as soon as he was picked up from school. To this day, I celebrate that my little Black boy loved reading so much he literally wanted to read all the time.

It is my hope more parents will expose their children to the library and reading as much as possible, particularly our Black and Brown children. By doing so, undoubtedly, this will help with decreasing the summer slide, increasing their achievement levels and closing learning gaps more rapidly once they return to school, post summer. I am fully aware some may not be able to visit the library regularly, as it may not be feasible for them to do so. However, there are an abundance of donated books from local charitable organizations, low-cost books and electronic books available to serve a similar purpose.

It is imperative for educators to continue to work and to ensure Black and Brown students are exposed to equitable opportunities and resources. We cannot avoid addressing causes, risk factors, and racial disparities threatening the academic success of our students.

Where there has been this notion of a summer slide, there may now be a much broader slide as a result of the long-term challenges presented by the pandemic and many Black and Brown students will undoubtably experience increased learning gaps as a result. One reason being the lack of resources for some students, the stress, the isolation, and possible depression. Additionally, because of video footage being circulated, showing students sleeping during their virtual classes or worse, because of inappropriate private matters being exposed during the sessions, some students may suffer from long-term distress.

Furthermore, several parents have shared with me that virtual learning has posed problems for their student because some of the material was difficult to grasp virtually, and these parents felt ill-prepared to assist their student. Many parents continued to work and have been unavailable to assist with their learning goals. For Black and Brown students, this has created situations where some may have fallen even further behind their counterparts and extended the achievement gaps.

Students with learning disabilities and those who have Individual Educational Plans (IEP) are at an even greater risk during the pandemic, as their services may not have been delivered with fidelity in the usual customary manner of the face-to-face contact that the brick-and-mortar schools offer. Because the pandemic has forced distance learning, the potential decrease in the achievement gap will possibly mirror those of the summer slide or disturbingly, create even larger gaps.

Schools must be strategic in their approaches to teaching during perilous times. I firmly believe that schools will need to employ innovative and nontraditional strategies in order for our students to regain lost knowledge and curve the gap developing for many. I also believe some of those strategies should include additional tutoring sessions and creative ways to engage students such as virtual collaborative learning.

As some students have transitioned back to school while others remain virtual, I have been solicited for my input by community leaders who are equally concerned about how to best support our underprivileged Black and Brown students in our community during these tumultuous times. I have assisted by providing advice and working collaboratively with the team to come up with meaningful solutions to ensure struggling minority students receive an extra layer of support. The goal is to help provide students with extended learning opportunities to assist with closing their learning gaps. Our aim is to provide measures to prevent students from falling any further behind.

The difficulties students experienced accessing their virtual courses, particularly at the onset of the massive online learning process, have been troublesome. Since our working group was fully aware that some parents within our targeted group did not have the financial means to purchase laptops or compatible bandwidth, the team and I continued to work on providing them with these items at no expense to their parents.

Effective interventions must be implemented and readily available to students.

If students need additional support, be sure to:

1. Ask the guidance counselor for support if the student is struggling academically, emotionally, or mentally.
2. Have your student attend teacher help sessions outside of the regular class time.
3. Contact local churches, community groups, or local and national organizations if you need assistance with purchasing laptops or internet connections.
4. Reach out to various community groups for extended learning opportunities for students who need additional academic help or assistance.
5. Contact the following organizations for additional support:

   • National Center for Children in Poverty
   • The National Urban League
   • Kids in Need Foundation
   • StandUp for Kids

- The Assistance League

There is no doubt that the "new normal" of distance and virtual learning has been overwhelming in general, but we need to ensure inequalities for accessing learning material is leveled across the board for all students. Black and Brown families are no strangers to fighting for equal access and the pandemic has brought about new obstacles for us to overcome.

Ultimately, we cannot allow our Black and Brown students to fall short of their learning goals but to resist similar results of the summer slide. Hopefully, we won't face another pandemic or school closures to this degree ever again, and therefore, virtual learning will remain a choice for students and not a mandatory order for those who do not learn best this way, particularly Black and Brown students from the lower socioeconomic backgrounds. Needless to say, we must be prepared to offer them maximum support if such a need arises again because unquestionably most students will be impacted by required virtual and distance learning, but our Black and Brown students will suffer the most.

"Education is about empowerment, about cultivating a human being to the highest possible potential—a tool for fulfilling the immensity of Being."

❧

Sadhguru

CHAPTER 9

Utilizing Extracurricular Activities as Incentives

During my adolescent years, I was sure to show respect for persons of authority and I refrained from having discipline issues by following school rules. Involvement in extracurricular activities was an integral part of my daily schedule, serving as an additional motivating factor to excel. Innately, I wanted to perform well, but being involved in a variety of activities on campus motivated me to do my best in the classroom. It may sound far-fetched but knowing I could participate in the extracurricular activities brought me tranquility and comfort. It also provided me with additional opportunities to engage with peers in an environment where we celebrated and supported each other.

My basketball coach once told the team our grades were priority and if we did not earn acceptable grades, we could not remain on the team. As a teen, I did not understand the correlation between earning proficient grades and playing a sport. I was oblivious to the state having specific requirements and if anyone scored below a 2.0 grade point average, they were not allowed to participate in any extra-curricular activities. As a result of my first-hand experiences, my love for sports and school activities, I understand the importance of encouraging students to get involved in extracurricular activities. My experiences with young adults further demonstrated that when most students are connected to a sport or club, it builds character, commitment, teamwork, and their grades and attendance improves. When a student builds on all the afore-mentioned, it certainly provides a platform for them to succeed in the classroom.

Consequently, it was no surprise when I served as assistant principal at the middle school, the majority of students who ex-perienced discipline issues had no connection to a school group or organization. To the contrary, the students who participated in sports or other extracurriculars, experienced much fewer disciplinary issues. The realization that misconduct would curtail their participa-tion in activities they valued, served as an encouraging factor for them to behave in school and perform at an acceptable academic level. There is a plethora of activities at the secondary level such as student government, various clubs, and community organizations students can find to interest them.

To my point, involvement in school activities in some capacity can help to provide students incentives and motivate them to actually want to attend school. Although, some students' main reason for attending school may not be because of academic engagement, but simply being in school helps them by the mere fact they are in an educational setting. Surely, they will absorb a certain degree of knowledge, even if it's not their intention. Additionally, in order to participate in extracurricular activities, students are required to maintain at least average grades. I am by no means advocating for students to come to school solely because of extracurriculars, but I have encountered students whose home lives are so disheveled that the only consistent, family-like connection they have is with their teammates. I, however, have used extracurriculars as a motivating factor for my students to maintain passing grades and to curtail discipline issues.

To demonstrate how being involved in extracurricular activities on campus can potentially impact a student's life in a positive manner, I would like to share a story passed on to me by a colleague about a young Black female student, we will call Tracy, whose distressed home life spilled over into her school life. Tracy's parents were not involved in her life, she resided with her older sibling. She was a transfer student and began getting into a great deal of trouble shortly after arriving on campus. For instance, she regularly spewed profanities at her teachers, had no regard for authoritative figures, and was often in perpetual discord and physical altercations with her peers. The principal was alerted by an assistant of Tracy's constant misconduct because Tracy exhibited behavior that could potentially lead to serious problems for herself and others.

In addition to the assistant principal's concerns, the basketball coach shared that Tracy was an outstanding player but was disrespectful, insubordinate, and sowed discord with her team members. The coach also stated he had cautioned Tracy that if her poor behavior continued, he would restrict her from participating and/or she would face removal from the team altogether. After hearing from the assistant principal, the coach, and several of Tracy's peers, the principal decided she would make a deliberate effort to speak with Tracy personally, in hopes it would curtail her defiant and unruly behavior.

As the principal approached Tracy, she visibly displayed signs of anger by screaming and directing profane language at the principal. Additionally, she screamed for the principal not to come near her as she walked away rapidly in the opposite direction. The principal removed herself from Tracy's personal space but remained persistent in her efforts to calm her from a distance. It was apparent that Tracy would find herself in the discipline office if she did not alter her behavior. Yet, she continued to be highly disobedient and rebellious. Administrators were accustomed to students becoming angry and displaying unruly behavior at times, but the principal was startled as Tracy continued to yell uncontrollably and showed signs of distressed breathing. With no visible trigger, she turned and approached the adults present in a threatening manner, made obscene gestures, and showed no signs of calming down. The principal and I held similar beliefs as it related to suspensions, which was, suspending students from school was a last resort because there are significant advantages to keeping students on campus when they are facing punitive outcomes. Obviously, there are times when an out-of-school suspension is warranted and unavoidable. In this case, the student refused to comply with any directives given to her by several administrators and was creating a school disruption. In the end, there appeared to be no other choice than to approve Tracy's suspension from school, a punishment typically reserved for the most extreme situations.

In addition to Tracy's imminent school suspension, she was removed from the basketball team as a result of this incident and prior misconduct. Once Tracy realized she would not be permitted to remain on the basketball team, her behavior completely changed. She apologized profusely for her actions to the principal, the coach, and the others involved in this incident. Surprisingly, she actually pleaded with the coach to reinstate her back on the team while displaying a distressful cry. Because of Tracy's "I don't care" demeanor and the bad girl image she displayed in the presence of her peers, the principal was quite flabbergasted Tracy had humbled herself to relentlessly self-advocate.

Principals have all witnessed students who, after a display of wrongdoing or volatile behavior, will later show regret for their actions, but there was something different about how this young lady desperately pleaded for forgiveness and to remain on the team. Per school policy, the school phoned Tracy's guardian to remove her from campus, but when she arrived, she requested to meet with both the principal and the basketball coach. During the meeting, Tracy's older sibling also pleaded with the coach to allow her to remain on the team. She explained that basketball was the only activity that motivated Tracy and she was afraid that she would lose her altogether if she was removed from the team.

Tracy's behavior rose to the level of egregiousness, and it was highly inappropriate. Disappointingly, she had acted in such a way to warrant immediate corrective strategies to assist her in understanding the significance of her actions. As a result, Tracy was indeed suspended from school. When she returned, she once again, apologized passionately and courageously and continued to advocate for herself about remaining on the basketball team and showed remorse for her wrongdoings.

Tracy unwaveringly declared to alter her behavior, and her pledge to discontinue her misconduct was believable. The principal pondered the situation, reflected on the conversation with Tracy's sister, and concluded the benefits of Tracy remaining on the team far exceeded her being removed but the final decision belonged to the coach. It is best practices to support coaches and allow them autonomy to make the decisions for their team members, particularly in instances such as this.

This was a delicate conversation because, although the principal believed she would be providing a unique opportunity in Tracy's favor, she expressed to the coach she would support whatever decision he made. In the end, the coach decided to allow Tracy another opportunity to prove herself and all together, the adults planned to use basketball as a means for Tracy to improve her behavior and grades. After all, there was no reason she couldn't be a successful student, her academic data revealed she was more than capable with proper interventions.

Tracy went on to complete the season in good standing without any other substantial discipline issues. It was apparent to the administrative team that she was serious about altering her tumultuous past. Providing Tracy with another opportunity to prove herself was a gamble that paid off.

As evidenced by this story, educators must sometimes take a detour from normal disciplinary procedures, if the deviation potentially supports the student's path to success. This is particularly true if a student appears to understand the ramifications of their actions or misconduct. Yet, it can sometimes be difficult to discern when a student is being sincere about wanting to make a positive change which makes it more difficult to make these cumbersome decisions.

I shared the previous story about Tracy to reveal how sports or other extracurricular activities can be an instrumental force keeping a student motivated to attend school. I am convinced if this student was not allowed to remain on the team, she perhaps would have spiraled out of control, but instead her longing to participate in an extracurricular activity, annihilated her desire to misbehave. After reflecting on this story, I realize there were a number of factors, i.e., the support, camaraderie, and just feeling like she belonged to a unit, ultimately contributed to Tracy's eventual graduation. This situation in particular is one resonating with me as it relates to a student's desire to be connected to something outside of the classroom. This story concludes with Tracy graduating. Nonetheless, we will never know explicitly if she would have experienced a similar outcome if it had not been for her relentless self-advocacy and her longing to stay connected to something so enormously important to her. As a village, it is our responsibility to encourage students' interests by exposing, and ultimately, connecting them to out-of-class activities whenever possible.

"When we see the face of a child, we think of the future. We think of their dreams about what they might become, and what they might accomplish."

Desmond Tutu

CHAPTER 10

The Invisible Student

T he term "invisible" is unequivocally not a term that one should want to associate with any student. However, during my stint as a middle school principal, concerns were divulged to me by a team member about a particular cohort of students sliding under the radar because of their mediocre academic and behavioral classifications. As I listened intently to the comments of the team member, I learned those students were performing academically in the range of a 2.0 - 2.9 on a 4.0 scale. Fortunately, most of those students were not displaying inappropriate behaviors, yet, those students were in a fragile position. The main point of trepidation became clear, which was those students were positioned to easily tumble into the undesirable category of academic failure. The reason was because there was little space for a decrease in their grades without them falling below the state's established standard proficiency, which is a 2.0 grade point average.

I was intrigued with the information presented to me regarding my students on the imaginary academic border line. Consequently, I wanted to swiftly put a tourniquet on the issue to stop the flow of them falling through the proverbial cracks. Obviously, my primary responsibility as an administrator was to ensure every student received equitable, academic, and emotional support. When I served as a classroom teacher, providing the type of support my students needed was not a complicated task. My students were well abreast of the classroom procedures and the expectations I set for each of them. Subsequently, as an administrator, it was anticipated and vital I refocused my attention from a small group to the entire student body. That meant my every decision had to collectively encompass what was in the best interest for all students.

This newfound information from my colleague referred to students who performed academically at the mediocre level and were seldom in the administrative office for disciplinary issues. Those students became unwittingly labeled as "invisible students." Pedagogically speaking, if students perform within the C-grade range, it is typically quite easy for them to dip below the proficient level without much notice, given to their ill-fated decline. Moreover, if a student's overall grade point average falls below the 2.0 scale, they are at risk of failing and perhaps getting into disciplinary issues as a result of being academically unsuccessful. Furthermore, those students are at risk of losing hope and motivation or becoming detached from their school community.

It was difficult to accept my students were being labeled invisible students when slipping under the radar. Additionally, it was heartbreaking that they were routinely unnoticed. While some may believe the students going unnoticed is positive and might be an indication they are refraining from getting into trouble, comparable to the old adage "no news is good news." However, I beg to differ in this instance. School is never a place where students should go unnoticed. Quite the contrary, school is a place where we should illuminate the accolades of each student and provide him or her with incentives to continue to perform at his or her best and celebrate success.

In this case, incentives can be instrumental in ensuring students stay on track. Rewarding students for doing what is expected of them should not be treated as insignificant. Incentives are motivational enhancements. Common sense, and my years of experience in education, confirm that not all students receive the same amount of support outside of school. Some students actually attend school for the extra layer of support which feeds their emotional needs.

I was committed to working strategically for this population of students to influence the school's environment on their behalf in a positive manner. Additionally, I wanted them to have unsuppressed opportunities to enhance their academic standing through access to equitable resources and real-world experiences. With additional knowledge and a newfound realization, I was committed to putting emphasis on this demographic of students. I informed my assistant we needed to explore enhancement options for the invisible students and come up with a plan to support their rise above this unstable classification. A data guru team member produced the breakdown of the compiled data upon request, along with additional information to assist us in planning for these students.

To maximize the support for this delicate group, I committed to tracking their data. The tracking process included a regular review of their attendance and grades. I provided a list of students to the academic teams for them to track the progress of their specific students. We then met regularly to discuss any student we felt needed academic, behavioral, or emotional support, providing individualized interventions when applicable. I knew the importance of providing interventions and this was the main goal of tracking.

Next, I reviewed the academic programs in place prior to my arrival as principal. There were two there, with one of them designated for students demonstrating the highest academic achievement. It also required an application process for acceptance into the program. The other program was also established for honor students but required no application. The invisible students who were known as basic students, were not assigned to an academic program. Hence, they were not being recognized, educationally tracked, or receiving intrinsic rewards in the way their peers were in the honors programs.

In an effort to change this, I continued meeting with teachers who were willing and committed to creating a third program for our invisible students. Setting the entire school on three programs meant all my students now belonged to a specific cohort, their own special peer group. I must emphasize though, this group was highly encouraged to elevate them-selves to the honors level. I knew the importance of each student feeling connected to a group, but I must admit, I underestimated how jubilant the once invisible students would be once their cohort was established. Almost immediately, I heard positive affirmations from the students. It gave me joy to see how they responded when they received special notes from their teachers. The students not only voiced their gratitude, their smiles showed that they welcomed the newfound attention.

In addition to tracking their progress and providing them with special notes, the team working specifically with this group of students, established field trips and invited special guest speakers to further motivate them. The desired outcome was to ensure the students felt special and were noticed for the good deeds they performed in our school community. These measures were put in place to enhance their grades and self-esteem. In this way, ensuring that students felt valued was not tied solely to a particular grade point average.

In addition to all such measures, I greeted each of my students at the front entrance as they entered the building. This was an opportunity for me to say something kind to each one of them or to give a compliment. I even observed students who barely uttered a word throughout the day, smile with exuberance when I engaged them in conver-sation or acknowledged them in some way. I would also encourage my more active students, before school and during lunch time, to sit with those who appeared to have no friends. I wanted each student to feel connected and to build relationships.

Of course, there will always be different layers of student academic performances, it's only natural. However, even those who struggle academically should never be referred to as invisible. There are ways to eliminate this undesired classification by targeting students with various layers of support. This includes, but is not limited to, involvement on campus, mentoring, regular counselor check-ins, and more.

At this school, we made specific and diligent efforts to protect our vulnerable student population falling into this category. On the basis of this experience, I recommend for parents and teachers to pay particular attention to students who are in this category to provide adequate support. We must all work to make sure there are no "invisible students." Their grades may represent average status, but we need to ensure that they know they are, by no means, average students. I am optimistic the term will vanish, and all students will have the opportunity to shine.

To further demonstrate the importance of challenging every student to their fullest potential, I share the story of Alicia who categorically believed she was an invisible student during middle and high school. Alicia stated she was never placed in an honors course or challenged much for that matter. While in school, Alicia did not feel smart. She considered honors courses to be hard classes and out of her league, and only for the really smart kids. With many of the same attributes and characteristics of an invisible student, Alicia performed as an average student while having no discipline issues. She didn't have very many friends and although she had satisfactory relationships with her teachers, Alicia did not feel a connection with them. Even with her mediocre grades and no clear direction, Alicia graduated high school. When many of the students were being recognized for their accomplishments during the senior awards events and graduation, her name was never called, which again made her feel invisible. After graduation, Alicia had little to no hope of attending college. Fortunately, she had a friend who was accepted into college and this friend convinced her to apply to an HBCU. To Alicia's surprise, she was accepted but apprehensive because she had not learned adequate study skills and felt that she would not be successful. Unfortunately, this became evident shortly after Alicia's first semester. She was placed on academic probation and this reminded her of the times she felt invisible while in high school. Since Alicia was at a smaller historically black college where the professors took a vested interest in her success, showing great concern, she was able to get back on track with a study plan developed for her. Alicia was determined and graduated. She then went on to pursue a master's degree. She explained that graduating from college with multiple degrees far exceeded the goals she thought she would ever achieve. She wants other students to not underestimate their potential or future opportunities. She feels that she exemplifies what an invisible student looks like but was able to overcome that barrier with a mother who wanted more for her, a friend who saw that she was capable of more, and a post-secondary educational institution that supported her while holding her to high expectations.

"Let us think of education as the means of developing our greatest abilities, because in each of us there is a private hope and dream which, fulfilled, can be translated into benefit for everyone and greater strength of our nation."

✧

John F. Kennedy

CHAPTER 11

My Career Chose Me and I Embraced it

A s I approach the conclusion of my book, I would be remiss if I did not include information related to my overall experience as an educator. As a whole, my educational career was gratifying. I began teaching immediately after graduating from college and right away I recognized I was destined to work with students in some capacity. I accepted my initial teaching position at a high school in Miami, FL and although anxious, enthusiastic, and a bit apprehensive, I enjoyed my first assignment. The school's demographics consisted mostly of kids of color, with the vast majority being of Hispanic descent.

I was a novice and eager young teacher in my early twenties, with my chronological age barely surpassing the ages of my bright and overzealous students. Nevertheless, I understood the importance of presenting myself in a professional manner and to not fraternize with the students beyond the normal, expected school activities. Therefore, I was certain to represent myself in a mature and appropriate manner at all times, ensuring there were no blurred lines. Yet, at the conclusion of one school day in particular, one of my male students sauntered into my classroom, positioned himself on one knee, and boldly asked me to attend prom with him. I was caught completely off guard and flabbergasted, but I responded swiftly by reminding him I was his teacher and not a peer. Slightly unnerved, I gently expressed to him that it would not be appropriate for me to do so and then I asked him to leave. However, before he exited the classroom, he alluded to guessing my age, without confirmation from me, and stated, "You can't be more than about two or three years older than I am, so what's the big deal?" While his assumption was accurate, and a bit endearing, I knew the significance of not entertaining his gesture. Thankfully, after this encounter ended, the student continued to show respect for my position and completed the school year without further incidents. Though my husband and I often chuckled about it, this is a story I share with many new teachers as they embark upon their careers, particularly if they are teaching at a high school with students close to their ages.

Although I thoroughly enjoyed my instructtional assignment in Miami, by choice, my position there would not extend beyond two and a half years. My husband was raised in Miami and decided he wanted to live elsewhere, perhaps a place a lot less hectic. Interestingly enough, my husband insisted I choose our next place of residence and I chose to return to the area where I was raised, Brevard County, FL.

Over the years, I reflected and remained perplexed about my decision to return to the town I was familiar with. After living in the progressive metropolitan city of Miami, returning to my hometown, a place the exact opposite, was peculiar to say the least. Nevertheless, I contemplated my decision and found I was determined to make a positive difference in my hometown community.

Upon relocating to Brevard County, there were no teaching job opportunities available in my certification area, which is Business Education. In the early 1990s, there was an ongoing pun, stating, if a person taught business, they never left the position until retirement, demise, or unique circumstances. Therefore, I accepted a part-time position as an adjunct professor at the local community college, and soon after, I taught at a secondary school in Orlando. This school was close enough for me to commute so my husband and I continued residing in Brevard County.

As I stated earlier, Business teachers rarely vacated their positions unless there was an unusual reason. Well, the unique situation occurred when randomly, my former Business teacher informed me she was getting married and as a result would take an early retirement. I was elated that an instructional position was now available at my alma mater, Titusville High School, in Titusville, FL. Incidentally, as it turned out, the principal at that time was my former history teacher, and therefore, he was familiar with my work ethics. I interviewed with him and he hired me after I completed my contract in Orlando.

Accepting this position brought about numerous emotions, as I would now be a teacher at the high school I once attended. A place where most of my experiences were favorable and the same school that propelled me to become an advocate for myself at an early age. My memorable teaching career at Titusville High School spanned over 16 years. Throughout that time, I was able to amass indelible relationships with my students. My classroom was inundated with kids before and after school because students felt comfortable speaking and visiting with me. I was, and still am, referred to by many of them as "Mama Jones." I shared mutual admiration with my students and the relationships I built with them are permanent.

During my time as a teacher there, I also became the first Black teacher of the year at Titusville High School in 1997. Teaching brought me so much joy that quite honestly, I never fathomed I would ever leave the classroom until retirement. However, I was being tugged by my desire and ambition to become an educational leader. I wanted so desperately for my own children, and all the children of color in my community, to have a Black female role model in the educational field. There were, and still are, few Black and Brown leaders in the county in which I worked. Hence, after great contemplation concerning whether I would continue as a teacher or advance my career, I ultimately left the classroom to become the assistant principal of discipline at the local middle school.

I served as assistant principal there for four years and next, I assumed a position as the curriculum assistant principal at a different middle school in the same district. The following school year, the position as principal of Jackson Middle School became available. I applied and soon after, I was appointed. Accepting the position now meant there were two Black principals in the city of Titusville, and this had never happened before. It was a considerable reach, particularly because we were both Black females. As one would expect, the position did not come without manageable challenges. Nevertheless, I considered the career advancement a milestone for me and those who yearned for more people of color to be visible in our community. I was content to serve in this capacity for our students of color, as well as for all kids, to see Black females display the intellect, capability, and propensity to serve as educational leaders in areas of the country so sparse in this specific representation.

Once I became principal of the middle school, I reflected how the child placed in the lowest phase class possible in 9th grade, was now a principal. After the 9th-grade experience I faced, high expectations became the rule for me and not the exception. I declared to work to ensure my students would be challenged to their fullest potential. This meant, as an educational leader, I was determined to set high expectations for myself, my faculty, and without a doubt, for my students. There is no secret that being a Black female leader with high standards is not welcomed by all and often met with great resistance by many. Nevertheless, I took my responsibilities seriously and I was determined that my students would be provided a quality education and have every opportunity to live up to their fullest educational potential.

"Education is the key to unlocking the world, a passport to freedom."

Oprah Winfrey

CHAPTER 12

Education is the Key

"The function of education is to teach one to think intensively and to think critically. Intelligence plus character—that is the goal of true education."
Dr. Martin Luther King, Jr.

I began this book by speaking about the inequities I experienced as it related to my education and lower socioeconomic status as a youth. What I did not share was that I set a goal to become the principal of that very same school, Titusville High School in Titusville, FL. Incredibly, I achieved my goal in the summer of 2017, when I was appointed as the first and only Black female high school principal in the school district. I must acknowledge the late Mr. Harry T. Moore, who served as principal of the Titusville Negro School in the 1930s, and for opening the door for me to have the opportunity. Mr. Moore was a local civil rights activist who fought for equality and paved the road for me and many other African Americans in the field of education. I am eternally grateful for his sacrifices.

As principal, there were two specific accomplishments I am most satisfied with. First, within two years, the overall graduation rate increased by more than five percent. Secondly, the suspension rate decreased substantially, particularly for Black males. In addition, as I was literally finishing this last chapter, I received word that Titusville High School was ranked amongst the "Best High Schools" in our nation. (USnews.com) The information collected and used to calculate this distinction was based on data from the 2017-18 school year, which was during my tenure as principal. Titusville High School ranked 6078 out of the nearly 18,000 high schools that were considered. Hence, I was fortunate to work with an amazing, diverse group of students, and they are to be commended for this accomplishment. This ranking takes into consideration outcomes for college readiness, college curriculum breadth, reading and math proficiency and performance, underserved student performance, and the graduation rate. I am elated that the high standards my team and I set contributed to those scores. This acknowledgement further demonstrates our team's efforts to ensure our students received a quality education. Though I was not able to physically rejoice with them since I had recently retired, I nonetheless celebrated this accomplishment in spirit.

My resolve to ensure the implementation of high educational standards, supporting extracurricular activities, and building relationships with my students were core priorities. It was paramount that I protected their instructional time while providing them with memorable after-school events. Hence, it was important to me that my students were aware of my vested interest in their general welfare, during and after school. On countless occasions, and with exuberance, my students often voiced their gratitude to me for attending their various events. The enthusiasm they displayed as a result of my presence at those activities carried over into my daily interactions with them. This is evidenced by the frequent cheerful greetings and joyful hugs I received from them. Such experiences have confirmed for me that genuine relationships are essential when trying to persuade students to embrace opportunities, potentially leading to their successes. I shall continue to devote time to mentoring and encouraging our youth and young adults to pursue their education productively and with resilience.

In general, Black and Brown students face tremendous obstacles, certainly more than their counterparts. However, equipped with the proper tools, resources, and a steadfast support system, our students do well to avoid unwelcome and unnecessary struggles.

Unquestionably, the village must continue to encourage, challenge, and prepare more students of color for their saunter across the high school graduation stage as they embark upon the plethora of post-secondary opportunities awaiting them.

"Greatness is not measured by what a man or woman accomplishes, but by the opposition he or she has overcome to reach his goals."

Dorothy Height

FINAL WORDS

The primary focus of this book was providing Black and Brown students with educational information to challenge and encourage them to reach their fullest potential. Though, of course, I have always cherished teaching and supervising ALL students, regardless of their ethnicity. I have a special place in my heart for students whom society, or their home situations, puts at a disadvantage, as well as for any students who struggle. I hope this book will inform and inspire students, parents, and educators alike. However, even if my suggestions and experiences help only one person conquer a challenge, or overcome an obstacle because of my advice, then I have succeeded. Although, it is my hope and desire for many to find this book a useful resource and tool while navigating through the educational system.

"From Poverty to Principal" has been an incredible journey, to say the least. Clearly, becoming a principal as a double minority in the south, where diversity is not prevalent, would not have been possible without my commitment to secure a solid education.

Achieving my goal came with some challenges and resistance, which of course, are welcomed by no one, but I asked myself the proverbial question, "If not me, then who?"

God continues to grant me many remarkable opportunities and I have been abundantly blessed. Now, I welcome the next chapter in my life in which I hope to fulfill my mantra, which is to live a faith-filled life, using my experience and passion to inspire others. One means of fulfilling my mantra shall be to continue working with youths and young adults, promoting positive self-esteem, self-confidence, preparing them for leadership roles, and mostly to encourage them to believe in themselves, while acknowledging the struggles of the past and the uncertainties lying ahead. It is also my desire to aid others in rising above poverty. Education is the key to doing so.

As I close, I share with you my deep desire to bring others on the mission with me to expand the boundaries and empower students to become advocates for their education. The future is enormously bright for our youth and young adults of color, but we must work collectively to provide them with constructive guidance, unceasing encouragement, and unobstructed educational experiences.

"Education is the most powerful weapon which you can use to change the world."

Nelson Mandela

POINTS TO PONDER
For Parents

POINT TO PONDER #1

On a scale of 1-10, how do you rate your involvement in your student's educational process?

Suggestions:
- Contact the teacher at least once a semester via e-mail, phone call, or other means.
- Know the classroom behavioral expectations.
- Become familiar with the teacher's course syllabus.
- Become active in the parent-teacher organization or the school advisory council.
- Attend your student's after-school events regularly.
- Be available and visible.

POINT TO PONDER #2

If your student is struggling academically, do you know who to reach out to?

Suggestions:
- Talk with your student to ascertain the specific struggle.
- The teacher should be your first school contact.
- Allow the teacher an opportunity to explain the difficulties your student is experience-ing.
- Going to the administration for an issue your student is having in class should only come after you have spoken with the teacher or if there is a situation that warrants going to the next level.
- Ask about tutoring or after-school help sessions and ensure that your student attends.
- Meet with the counselor to see if they have any additional resources to support your student.
- Locate support resources.

POINT TO PONDER # 3

Have you reviewed your student's transcript recently? Do you review it annually?

Suggestions:

- Meet with the counselor and ask that he or she thoroughly explain the transcript to you.
- Ask for a copy of your student's transcript at the end of each school year and review it with your student.
- Review your student's tests data annually.
- Discuss the number of credits your student needs each semester with the counselor.
- Ensure that your student is in the proper courses. Course placements can make a tremendous difference in the educational process for students.
- Talk with your student about career options to confirm that the courses they select, align with that choice.
- If your student is short on credits or qualifies for grade forgiveness, consider summer school.

POINT TO PONDER #4

Does your student know how much you value education? Do you model how important education is?

Suggestions:
- Do you talk about the importance of education with your student on a regular basis?
- Spend more time reading instead of watching TV.
- Establish specific study times for your student.
- Purchase books as gifts for your student.
- Take your student on educational field trips, such as the museums or nature tours.

POINT TO PONDER #5

Who do you contact if your student experiences any discipline issues at school? What process do you use to support your student or your student's school?

Suggestions:

- Equitable consequences for students of color has been a long-standing issue. Be sure to hear your student's perspective as well as the educator's.
- Ask your student to provide you full details of any situation in which they receive punishment or consequences.
- Follow up with the adult who addressed the issue with your student to be sure the consequence aligns with the infraction.
- If your student committed the infraction, be sure to hold them accountable for their actions and support the school's corrective strategy if you believe it is fair and equitable.

POINT TO PONDER #6

Is it difficult for you to access a phone during the workday?

Suggestions:
- Provide multiple ways of contact for the school to reach you. In times of emergency, often parents will list the mother and father as the first contact.
- List the person first who is the easiest to reach in the event there is a true emergency.
- Set clear expectations for those on your emergency contact list.

POINT TO PONDER #7

How are you working to create a partnership with your student's teachers?

Suggestions:
- Establish a professional relationship with the teacher and ensure regular and on-going communication.
- Attend parent night and teacher conferences.
- E-mail several times a year to check the status of your student.
- Teachers are more apt to respond quicker with parents when they know the parents are highly involved in their student's educational process.

POINT TO PONDER #8

Is your student struggling with learning as a result of distance learning due to the COVID-19 pandemic or other extreme issues? How will you work to keep your student from falling behind or experiencing a learning gap?

Suggestions:
- Consider taking your student to the library regularly.
- Consider reading with your student regularly. If your students are older, require them to do additional learning activities outside of class.
- Monitor your student's progress more closely. I suggest weekly updates from the teacher if they are struggling.

POINT TO PONDER #9

How familiar are you with graduation requirements?

Suggestions:
- Become familiar with the state assessment your student will be required to pass before graduation.
- Know the grade point average your student must maintain in order to be considered in good standing and be allowed to participate in extracurricular activities.
- Meet with the counselor to ensure your student is taking the proper courses.
- Be sure your student is taking the required core courses (math, science, social studies, and English).
- Be sure your student takes the correct elective courses as it relates to graduation and to their post-secondary interest.

POINT TO PONDER #10

Who do you contact if your student shows signs of a learning disability?

Suggestions:
- Speak with the teachers and the counselor to share your concerns. Ask if they have seen signs of academic struggles.
- Request an evaluation for your student.
- Track your student's daily behavior for later discussions.
- Keep an open line of communication with your student about their learning needs.

POINT TO PONDER #11

Does your student exhibit signs of being an invisible student?

Suggestions:
- Are your student's grades consistently averaging between 2.0 - 2.9?
- Does your student talk about not getting acknowledged by his/her teachers?
- Does your student eat alone at school or talk to you about who they eat lunch with or spend time with at school?

POINT TO PONDER #12

Do your student's grades hover at average but they don't spend a great deal of time studying?

Suggestions:
- Consider placing them in accelerated courses, i.e., honors, advanced placement or dual enrollment for more rigor.
- Additional study time should easily enhance their grades, if not, speak with the teacher or counselor about providing more academically challenging courses.
- Hold your student to high standards and expectations.

POINT TO PONDER #13

Does your student qualify for free or reduced lunch based on your income? Are you sure they are eating at school each day?

Suggestions:
- Oftentimes, students of lower socio-economic status who qualify for free or reduced lunch refuse to sign up for this assistance because they are embarrassed.
- Ensure that you or your student submits the required information to receive free or reduced lunch.
- Some students will forgo lunch in order to keep their peers from knowing that they receive free or reduced lunch. Check with your student and encourage them to utilize their resources.
- Some students will claim to not be hungry in order to avoid the possibility of being embarrassed. Please make sure this is not happening to your student.

POINT TO PONDER #14

Many Black and Brown students who have reached high school never get a chance to visit a college campus. How many times have you taken your student to visit a college campus?

Suggestions:
- Arrange for your student to visit a college campus and if possible, take another student who might otherwise not have this opportunity.
- Middle school is a great time to expose them to higher learning. By high school, they should start to narrow their choices.
- If possible, parents should learn and guide their students to gain a better understanding of the college education process.

Exceptional Student Education Contributors

<u>Jana Stokes</u>
ESE Advocate
Mother of a special need's child
Founder for Ryan's Gift of Advocacy
Former Teacher

<u>Ruth Gary</u>
Retired ESE Educator (38 years)
Former College Professor
Irlen Syndrome Certified
Mentor

RESOURCE PAGE

- fldoe.org
- cde.state.co.us/cdelib/summerslide
- ed.gov
- khanacademy.org
- ncld.org
- urban.org
- understood.org
- kidshealth.org/en/parents/504-plans

Annetha Chambers Jones, Ed.S.

A retired middle and high school principal, educator, mentor, inspirational speaker, and author. Her professional accomplishments include being named as 1997 Teacher of the Year, 2010 Outstanding Assistant Principal of the Year, and a nomination for 2016 Principal of the Year. She created and implemented two mentoring programs which serviced more than 300 students in her community. Annetha is a member of several professional organizations, as well as an active member in her sorority, Delta Sigma Theta Sorority, Incorporated, where she donates her time to support others. A fun fact is that she competed in the Mrs. Florida pageant in 2001 and was selected as a top twelve finalist. She is proudly an HBCU graduate of "the" Florida A&M University. In addition, she obtained both a master's and a Specialist degree from Nova Southeastern University. Although Annetha retired in 2019, she remains certified in Educational Leadership, School Principalship, and Business Education.

Annetha's goal is to live a faith-filled life, while inspiring others through the passion of her voice. One of her main goals is to promote educational equality while providing encouragement and mentorship for young leaders of color to overcome obstacles and barriers too often placed before us. Annetha provides inspirational messages to various groups.

If you would like to have Annetha speak with you or your group, contact her at: www.annethajones.com